CW01066954

IVE PLAYS FROM ITV   ES

STARTING
OUT

Written by Anthony Horowitz

Notes and activities by John L. Foster

Hodder & Stoughton

LONDON SYDNEY AUCKLAND TORONTO

Acknowledgements

The publishers would like to thank the following for permission to reproduce material in this volume: John Agard for 'Stereotype'; Husson Productions for the poem from *Starting Out* by Horowitz and Foster; *Woman and Home* for 'Alison's Story', May, 1987; *Woman's Own* for 'The Greenhouse Effect', 24 July 1989.

Every effort has been made to trace and acknowledge ownership of copyright. The publishers will be glad to make suitable arrangements with any copyright holders whom it has not been possible to contact.

All enquiries re performance and ancillary rights should be addressed to: Contracts and Copyright Department, Central Independent Television plc, Central House, Broad Street, Birmingham B1 2JP.

No performance may be given unless permission has first been obtained.

British Library Cataloguing in Publication Data
Horowitz, Anthony
 Starting out.
 I. Title
 822'.914

 ISBN 0 340 52779 X

First published 1990

This book is based on scripts from the fifth *Starting Out* television series, produced by Geoff Husson Productions for Central Independent Television plc.
Scripts © 1989 Anthony Horowitz and Central Independent Television plc
Activities © 1990 John L. Foster
Central logo © 1989 Central Independent Television plc

All rights reserved. No part of this publication may be reproduced or transmitted in any form or by any means, electronic or mechanical, including photocopy, recording, or any information storage and retrieval system, without permission in writing from the publisher or under licence from the Copyright Licensing Agency Limited. Further details of such licences (for reprographic reproduction) may be obtained from the Copyright Licensing Agency Limited, of 33–34 Alfred Place, London WC1EW 7DP.

Typeset by Tradespools Ltd, Frome, Somerset
Printed for the educational publishing division of Hodder and Stoughton Ltd, Mill Road, Dunton Green, Sevenoaks, Kent by Richard Clay Ltd, Bungay, Suffolk

Contents

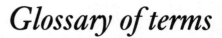

Glossary of terms

V/O	voice over
INT.	interior scene
EXT.	exterior scene
CUE TO	cut to
DISSOLVE TO	gradual transition from one shot to another
WIDE ANGLE	literally, a 'wide' or 'broad' shot.

From the author

When I was asked to write eight half-hour screenplays for the
television series 'Starting Out', my first thought was to refuse. I liked
the director – Geoff Husson – and it would have paid well, but I was
uneasy for three reasons.

First, it isn't the sort of thing I normally do. Most writers working in
TV and film are pigeon-holed to an extent. Even if their names are
seldom known to the public, they are known to the producers who
make (and find the money for) the programmes. Now, my 'field' is
comedy and fantasy: 'Robin of Sherwood', 'The Saint', 'William Tell'.
So what was I doing in hard-edged social realism, which is what these
plays were meant to be about?

Worse still, the more I thought about it, the more I found myself
wondering if I had anything constructive to say. After all, what is there
to say about racial prejudice or unemployment or drug abuse that
hasn't been said a hundred times already? But these subjects had to
appear in the plays because that's what Central TV wanted. Certainly,
we never touched on them in 'Robin of Sherwood'.

Finally, I had a problem with the whole idea of television being used
in education in all – not a great start when you're working for the
education department of a television network. At my own school,
television was never mentioned in polite conversation. Is it a cop-out to
watch TV for half an hour and then talk about what you've seen? If it
isn't, why do you need to have a programme written specially for
schools? After all, you can find a broad range of social issues in
'EastEnders', 'The Bill' – even 'Neighbours'.

I am not convinced that television has ever actually taught anyone
anything. Of course, it has a huge and immediate impact. You only
have to look at the millions that it has raised with its comic relief and
telethons for proof of that. But there is so much television flooding in
and flooding out. So much of television is basic and brainless –
gameshows, situation comedies, soaps, more gameshows. And
television is so easy to ignore, as it drones on in that corner of the living
room, that even the most beautifully made nature programmes, or the
most intricate political analysis, just becomes more flotsam and jetsam
on the endless flood of electrons.

Also, I asked myself, how can I offer my work for serious study when
I know that so much of its is based on cheating and lying?

Screenwriters cheat because if we showed life as it really is, nobody
would watch a single programme. Think about a day in your own life –
or even one hour. You get out of bed. You go to the toilet. You clean

1

our teeth. Fourteen police cars screech to a halt outside the front door. . . except they don't. And on TV, policemen don't get up, go to the toilet, etc.' because that's boring, and if you don't give your audience something exciting soon they're going to turn over or turn off. (In the USA, it has been said, the average viewer has an attention span of around eight seconds.)

So we cheat – except that we call it technique. We compress time. We put music in the background to trigger off the right emotion. We keep moving the camera to keep the eye amused. We cut out of scenes right at the best moment and move into the next ones when they're beginning to look interesting. We give our characters clever lines but we don't let them talk too long or else they'll slow up the action.

And gradually people come to think that what they are watching on television is some sort of truth, or at least a reflection of truth, and this is the big lie. If a place like Ramsay Street really existed, its inhabitants would surely be deported to a hospital for the hopelessly insane. Nobody behaves like that. A dead body on television does not look remotely like a dead body in real life. Every detail is a distortion, whether it's in fiction, in 'faction', or in fact.

So that was why I didn't want to do 'Starting Out'. But it was also the reason why, in the end, I did.

I decided to use the programme to look at television itself, to consider some of the questions I have just outlined. I wanted to write something that would make viewers think about the way that they were influenced by TV – and not just drama programmes, but commercials and news reporting, as well. I would use the most common and taken-for-granted format, the soap, and I would try to turn it on its head. I wouldn't just tell a story. I would also show *how* it was being told.

There is a story in these scripts – the friendship of Mike and Leo and their crime. I hope that story grips. But I've used a welter of effects that break into it, making it less real and therefore, hopefully, more open to question. These effects include captions, dream sequences, flashbacks, subtitles, voice overs, satire, parody and exaggeration. Finally, I even show the cameras pointing at the actors as they prepare to go home. These are all meant to say, 'this isn't true – it's TV drama', to make people think not just about the issues but how the issues are being presented.

And what about the issues? There again, I tried never to be obvious. The character of the garage owner is a crook and a racist. But I still tried to make him likeable. The old lady who is killed, on the other hand, is utterly loathsome. Karen is opposed to industrial pollution but still drives a car. And so on.

2

As to my other concern, my inexperience in this area, you can judge for yourself whether I have succeeded or not. When I was writing 'Starting Out', I talked to teachers, police officers, social workers, a magistrate, students, YTS workers and various pressure groups for ethnic minorities. I went to schools in the London borough of Stoke Newington, as well as in Lancashire, Birmingham and Milton Keynes. I tried, in other words, to adopt as broad a view as possible. Not just white. Not just London. Not just middle class.

But then, I was never trying to put a point of view that I considered right, just as there are surely no exactly right answers to the questions John Foster has added to these scripts. If people like what I have written, fine. But if they dislike them so much that they become angry and start putting forward their own points of view, maybe that's even better.

The scripts in this book are exactly as they were written for television. I have only made changes where it is necessary to fill in gaps in the story. There were eight programmes originally. For reasons of space only five are included here.

There are two important questions that I have often asked myself about the series.

Sally Williams is my favourite character in the series. She is just about the only character with no problems or hang-ups. She gets on with her day-to-day business, cooks meals, cleans the house, keeps the family going. She is a typical mother. In fact, I based her on my own mother (particularly her love of advertisements). To that extent, she is also the most realistic character in the plays. And I like – and believe in – her very straightforward point of view.

So why do most of the teachers I have met since the series went on air absolutely loathe her? They call her a 'stereotype' and accuse me of rampant sexism combined with no imagination. I have met teachers who have vetoed the whole series because of Sally Williams.

1 Is my mother a stereotype?

And the other missing question is this. Have you noticed how pleasantly all the characters speak? Compare the language in the programmes with the language in your own schools. Nobody says anything beginning with 'f'. Or 'w'. Or 's'... The reason for this is that nearly all the ugly language, the 'socially real' language, was censored by authorities who do not consider that young ears should be tainted by such vocabulary. In other words, although television would like you to believe in its characters, it would prefer them not to speak your language.

2 Is this hypocritical?

As far as I'm concerned, both questions lead to the same inescapable conclusion. In 'Starting Out', I tried to challenge the power and the influence of television. It was me *versus* TV. And I have a feeling, television won.

Anthony Horowitz

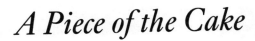

A Piece of the Cake

SCENE ONE

Int. Courtroom 10.00 a.m.

WE OPEN ON A *Magistrate* SITTING BEHIND A RAISED DAIS. SHE IS A WOMAN, IN HER FIFTIES, A BLUE-RINSED CONSERVATIVE. SHE WILL BECOME CENTRAL TO THE SERIES.

Magistrate   Michael James Williams. Will you please stand up?

CUT TO: REVERSE ANGLE. THE COURTROOM IS REPRESENTATIONAL RATHER THAN REALISTIC – ITS SIZE DISPROPORTIONATE TO THE AMOUNT OF PEOPLE IN IT. APART FROM A FEW (NON-SPEAKING) COURT PROFESSIONALS, WE WILL SEE *John* AND *Sally Williams* (*Mike's* PARENTS) AND *Sam Green*, CAREERS TEACHER AT *Mike's* SCHOOL. *Mike Williams* IS STANDING IN THE DOCK, A SMALL, NERVOUS FIGURE. LOST IN THE DARKNESS THAT SURROUNDS HIM.

CUT TO: RESUME ON *Magistrate*.

Magistrate   It is my duty to pass sentence on you, but before I do that, there is something I would like to say. Quite frankly, your entire case puzzles me.

CUT TO: CLOSE SHOT ON *John* AND *Sally*. *Sally* IS CLOSE TO TEARS. *John* COMFORTS HER.

Magistrate   [v/o] You come from a good family – with a comfortable house and a respectable background.

CUT TO: CLOSE SHOT ON *Green*. HE IS LISTENING WITH A SAD, 'I-TOLD-YOU-SO' SORT OF EXPRESSION.

Magistrate   [v/o] You went to a good school. . .

RESUME ON *Magistrate*.

Magistrate   [v/o] . . . and you had a good job, with every chance to build yourself a career.

CUT TO: CLOSE SHOT ON *Mike*. HE IS LISTENING, TIGHT-LIPPED AND PALE. IT'S HARD TO BELIEVE THAT THE *Magistrate* IS ACTUALLY TALKING ABOUT HIM.

Magistrate   [v/o] And yet you committed a serious and very cowardly crime.

SHE GESTURES AT A BULKY, DOG-EARED FILE.

Magistrate   I've read your social inquiry report, but I'm still puzzled. The facts are very straightforward. We all know *what* you did. But really ...

SHE SIGHS.

Magistrate   I just wish I could say I knew *why*.

CUT TO: OPENING CREDITS. THE CENTRAL MOTIF OF THE CREDITS IS A TYPICAL PHOTOGRAPHIC PORTRAIT OF THE *Williams* FAMILY – *John* AND *Sally, Karen, Michael* AND *Stephen. Mike* IS AT THE CENTRE. THE IMAGE SHATTERS.

CUT TO:

Captions

THE CAPTIONS ARE QUITE SEPARATE FROM THE CREDITS. THEY APPEAR, WHITE LETTERS ON A BLACK BACKGROUND.
CAPTION 1: AT THE AGE OF SIXTEEN ...
CAPTION 2: YOU CAN GET MARRIED. BUT YOU CAN'T CELEBRATE IN A PUB.
CAPTION 3: YOU CAN HAVE KIDS OF YOUR OWN. BUT YOU CAN'T SEE AN ADULT FILM.
CAPTION 4: YOU CAN LEAVE SCHOOL AND JOIN A TRADE UNION. BUT YOU CAN'T VOTE.
CAPTION 5: WHEN IS THE LAW GOING TO GROW UP?

CUT TO:

SCENE TWO

Int. Williams' home (kitchen) 8.30 a.m.

CLOSE SHOT: A BIRTHDAY CARD. THE NUMBER 'SIXTEEN' IS PROMINENT.

CUT TO: WIDER ANGLE. WE PULL BACK TO REVEAL BREAKFAST IN THE *Williams'* HOME – A MODERN, COMFORTABLE, WIMPEY-STYLE HOUSE. *Mike* IS SIXTEEN. HIS CARDS, JUST OPENED, ARE ON THE TABLE. *Mike* IS THE CENTRE OF ATTENTION, SURROUNDED BY HIS MOTHER AND FATHER AND HIS YOUNGER BROTHER, *Steve. John* PASSES *Mike* A PARCEL WRAPPED IN TEDDY BEAR PAPER.

John	Here you go, Mike.
Mike	Thanks, dad.
Steve	It's from me, too.
Mike	Yeah? You tight ...
Steve	I paid for the wrapping paper.
Mike	Teddy bears? I bet you chose it, too.
Steve	What's wrong with teddy bears?
Mike	Oh – I forgot. You sleep with one, don't you!
Steve	No, I don't.
Sally	Leave him alone!
Mike	[MOCKING] Oh, sorry! [TO Steve] Sorry, Stevie.
Steve	I don't sleep with a teddy bear.
Mike	No, of course not. You just talk to it before you go to sleep: 'Goodnight, teddy bear!' 'Goodnight, Stephen!'

Sally AND *John* ARE ABOUT TO INTERRUPT. *Mike* CUTS THEM OFF.

Mike	He does! I've heard him.
Sally	He's only fourteen.
Mike	Well, when I was fourteen I'd already discovered there were better things to sleep with than a cuddly toy.
Sally	Yes. Like hot water bottles.
Steve	[SARCASTIC] He's a real man!
John	Come on! Are you going to open it, or what?

Mike TURNS HIS ATTENTION BACK TO THE PARCEL – BUT WITH ONLY LIMITED ENTHUSIASM. THERE'S A SLOW FUSE BURNING UNDERNEATH THIS FAMILY CHIT-CHAT. AS HE STRUGGLES WITH THE SELLOTAPE, *John* CONTINUES.

John	I've got good news for you too, Mike. I had a word with Dave Pearson. He's the Personnel Manager at the QT-Pie Doll Factory.

Mike STOPS OPENING THE PARCEL. THERE'S A NOTE OF SUDDEN TENSION IN THE AIR.

Mike   Oh, yeah?

John   He's agreed to see you next week. [PAUSE] I thought you'd be pleased.

Mike   You could have asked me first.

John   Asked you? I'm doing you a favour!

Mike   Says who?

John   Use your eyes, Mike. You really think you've got any chance on your own? These days, it's not *what* you know that counts. It's *who* you know.

Sally   Your father's right, Mike.

Mike   Oh – he's always right, isn't he?

John   [PATIENTLY] We've talked about this, Mike. You know how it is around here. The steel's gone. The wool's gone. How many factories do you think there are? How many jobs?

Mike   But I don't want to work in a doll factory.

John   Oh – that's gratitude for you!

Sally   He is grateful. Aren't you, Mike?

John   Nineteen years of it hasn't done me any harm. Anyway, it can't hurt you to talk to him. You may learn a thing or two.

Mike   Like what?

John   Like it's not just a doll factory. QT-Pie dolls are the best selling range in Europe.

Sally   [QUOTING] 'They laugh. They cry. They wet themselves …'

John   There are QT-Pie clothes. QT-Pie accessories. QT-Pie cartoon books and feeding bottles. It's a big business, Mike … and with the sort of exam results you're going to get I wouldn't have said you had a lot of choice.

Mike   I don't have any choice, do I?

John   I just want the best for you, son. That's what any parent would want.

Mike   Yeah, thanks. But I'm sixteen now, right? I'm not a child any more. I can make up my own mind.

John IS ON THE EDGE OF ANGER, BUT HE DOESN'T WANT A ROW. HE AND HIS SON HAVE HAD TOO MANY ...

John   I'm only trying to help.

Mike   No. You're trying to make me into what *you* want me to be.

A DIFFICULT PAUSE. AS ALWAYS, *Sally* IS THE ONE WHO FILLS THE SILENCE.

Sally   You still haven't opened your present.

Mike TEARS THE REST OF THE PAPER OFF TO REVEAL AN EXPENSIVE WALLET WITH HIS INITIALS IN GOLD.

Mike   Thanks, very much. It's very nice.

Sally   It's real leather. Handstitched.

John   You'll be needing that soon – whatever you decide on. You'll be a wage-earner soon.

Steve   Or you can always keep your UB40 in it.

Sally   Stephen!

John TAKES OUT A FIVE-POUND NOTE AND HANDS IT TO *Mike.*

John.   Here you go, son. Something to start you off.

Mike TAKES THE MONEY, BUT HE IS UNEASY.

CUT TO:

SCENE THREE

Ext. Outside the Williams' home 9.00 a.m.

A NEWISH FORD ESCORT STANDS IN THE DRIVE. *John* IS LEAVING FOR WORK, DROPPING *Mike* AND *Steve* OFF AT SCHOOL ON THE WAY. *Sally* STANDS IN THE DOOR.

Sally   Now, you won't be late, will you! Karen's coming home with her new boyfriend, so it's going to be quite a party.

Steve PASSES THROUGH THE DOOR. AS HE GOES, HE BUNDLES A PAIR OF ICE-SKATES INTO HIS BAG.

Sally   Are you skating today, Steve?

Steve   If I've got time.

Sally   As long as you're home for tea.

Steve   Are you making a cake?

Sally   Wait and see.

> *Sally* KISSES *Steve. Mike* IS THE LAST TO LEAVE.

Sally   Try and have a nice day, dear. It is your birthday.

> *Mike* GIVES HER THE MEREST PECK OF A KISS AND CONTINUES.

John   Come on!

> CUT TO: CLOSE SHOT ON CAR. IT PULLS AWAY.

> CUT TO: RESUME ON *Sally*. SHE WATCHES THEM GO WITH JUST A HINT OF WORRY IN HER FACE. BUT SHE QUICKLY DISMISSES IT AND GOES BACK INTO THE HOUSE.

> CUT TO:

SCENE FOUR ▒▒▒▒▒▒▒▒▒▒▒▒▒▒▒▒▒▒▒▒▒

Ext. Mike's School 9.30 a.m.

> THE FORD ESCORT DRIVES OFF. *Mike* AND *Steve* WALK TOGETHER INTO THE SCHOOL. OTHER KIDS ARE ARRIVING FOR THE START OF THE DAY.

Steve   [SARCASTIC] What's up – Birthday Boy?

Mike   Oh, get off, Steve. You know it's not my birthday.

Steve   What do you mean?

Mike   It could have been last week. Or next week. Nobody knows. I don't have a *birth*day.

> *Steve* TWIGS. THE TWO OF THEM HAVE HAD THIS CONVERSATION BEFORE.

Steve   Yeah, I know. 'Cos you were adopted.

Mike   They just had to put a day on a form, that's all.

Steve   It's the same for me.

Mike   Do you ever think about who your mum and dad really were? Why they didn't want you?

Steve   Maybe they did want me. You don't know that.

Mike   Of course they wanted you. They really wanted you. That's why you were found wrapped in newspaper on a park bench …

Steve   It wasn't like that!

Mike TAKES PITY ON HIM.

Mike   Oh, come on! Don't start crying, for heaven's sake. I was just making a point – that's all.

Steve   What point?

Mike   The point that it doesn't make any difference. Sixteen, eighteen, twenty-one … who gives a monkey's? You know who I am.

CUT TO: ANOTHER ANGLE. *Mike* AND *Steve* STOP OUTSIDE THE MAIN SCHOOL BUILDING. THERE'S A DUSTBIN NEARBY.

Mike   Nobody. But they're trying to make me into somebody. Their somebody. This …

Mike TAKES OUT THE WALLET.

Mike   That's all they understand. Jobs. Money. But I don't want it. I just want to be me.

Mike THROWS THE WALLET INTO THE DUSTBIN AND STRIDES INTO THE SCHOOL. *Steve* WAITS A MOMENT, THEN FISHES IT OUT AGAIN. HE LOOKS INSIDE THE WALLET. IT IS EMPTY. HE CALLS AFTER *Mike*.

Steve   You've still kept the fiver!

CUT TO:

SCENE FIVE

Ext. QT-Pie Dolls Ltd 9.30 a.m.

John DRIVES THROUGH THE GATES OF A SMALL, FAMILY-RUN BUSINESS. IT'S AN OLD PLANT, PROBABLY VICTORIAN IN DESIGN. ON THE WALL THERE'S AN ADVERTISEMENT: 'QT-

PIE DOLLS LIMITED. THEY LAUGH, THEY CRY, THEY WET THEMSELVES'.

CUT TO:

SCENE SIX ▦▦▦▦▦▦▦▦▦▦▦▦▦▦▦▦▦▦▦▦▦▦▦▦▦▦▦

Ext QT-Pie Dolls Ltd (car park) 9.30 a.m.

CLOSE SHOT: *John* DRIVES INTO A CLEARLY DELINEATED SPACE – A WHITE RECTANGLE – THAT'S RESERVED, WITH HIS NAME AND RANK (SENIOR MANAGER).

CUT TO: WIDER ANGLE. ANOTHER MANAGER – *David Pearson* – HAS JUST GOT OUT OF HIS CAR IN ANOTHER RESERVED SPACE. *Pearson* IS A TWO-FACED, SELF-SERVING MAN IN HIS FORTIES. HIS NEAT, TIMID MANNER SUCCESSFULLY DISGUISES HIS RUTHLESSNESS.

Pearson	Good morning, John!
John	'lo, Dave.
Pearson	You had a word with your boy yet?
John	Yes. It's good of you to agree to see him.
Pearson	Not at all.
John	It's just that there've been a lot of rumours. Relocation. Redundancies. That sort of thing ...
Pearson	Rumours! Nothing to them ...
John	If you say so.
Pearson	I do.

HE HASTILY CHANGES THE SUBJECT.

Pearson	It's a great place this, John. To think that I started out twenty-two years back. I was in Despatch then. Ten years later I had my own car-parking space. Fifteen years and they gave me my own car ...
John	[INTERRUPTING] Dave – I have to tell you. Mike has a few reservations ...
Pearson	Kids these days! Don't know what's good for them. A

secure job with a chance to earn a few bob and a decent pension scheme ... what more do they want? Trouble is, they don't know. No sense of direction.

John [DOUBTFUL] That's true.

CUT TO: ANOTHER ANGLE. *John* AND *Pearson* WALK OFF TOGETHER, THEIR CONVERSATION FADING WITH THEM.

Pearson I love it here, John. I don't mind admitting it. It's my life. That's why I called my daughter Cutie.

John Right.

Pearson You send Steve to me ... I'll soon sort him out ...

John Actually, it's Mike ...

CUT TO:

SCENE SEVEN

Int. Williams' home (kitchen) 10.00 a.m.

CLOSE SHOT: THE RADIO IS ON IN THE BACKGROUND – A LOCAL STATION. *Sally* HUMS TO HERSELF AS SHE CLOSES THE DOOR OF THE DISH-WASHING MACHINE. ALL THE BREAKFAST THINGS ARE NEATLY STACKED.

CUT TO: WIDER ANGLE. THE KITCHEN HAS BEEN CLEANED AND TIDIED. *Sally* IS SURROUNDED BY ALL THE LATEST GADGETRY – FROM THE BLENDER TO THE MICROWAVE. SHE IS SMILING, AS SHE ALWAYS SMILES. A RADIO AD COMES ON AS SHE PREPARES THE BLENDER.

THE RADIO AD: MUSIC THROUGHOUT.

Male [v/o] Ooh! That looks good!

Female [v/o] Yes. It's a ready-made cake mix from Mr Bun, the baker. Just the thing for every happy family.

Male [v/o] Just add an egg and stir?

Female [v/o] That's right! It comes in chocolate, lemon, ginger, and new coffee and walnut flavour, too.

Male [v/o] Mmm! Smells delicious.

Female [v/o] Tastes even better. So remember the name.

Male [v/o] Mr Bun's ready-made cake mix.

Female [v/o] For happy families!

> CUT TO: ANOTHER ANGLE. *Sally* HAS GOT THE BLENDER READY. AT THE END OF THE AD, SHE OPENS A CUPBOARD AND TAKES OUT A PACKET OF 'MR BUN' – CHOCOLATE FLAVOUR. SHE DOES NOT BELIEVE IN THE WORLD OF FANTASY RADIO ADVERTISING, BUT USES IT AS A BENCHMARK AGAINST WHICH TO COMPARE HER OWN GOOD FORTUNE.

> CUT TO: CLOSE SHOT. THE TELEPHONE (ATTACHED TO THE WALL) RINGS.

> CUT TO: ANOTHER ANGLE. *Sally* TURNS DOWN THE RADIO ON HER WAY OVER TO THE TELEPHONE. SHE ANSWERS.

Sally Hello?

> CUT TO:

SCENE EIGHT

Int. Hospital 10.15 a.m.

> *Karen* IS A NURSE IN A GERIATRIC HOSPITAL. SHE'S MAKING THE CALL FROM A PUBLIC TELEPHONE IN A CORRIDOR. SHE IS TIRED AND OVER-WORKED. SHE HAS RUNG TO SAY THAT SHE CAN'T MAKE THE PARTY.

Karen Hello – mum? It's Karen ...

> CUT TO:

SCENE NINE

Int. William's home (kitchen) 10.15 a.m.

> AS BEFORE. FROM HERE, INTERCUT AS REQUIRED.

Sally Oh hello, dear. I was wondering when you'd call.

Karen Mum, I'm ringing about this evening ...

Sally   You are going to come, I hope. Mike's been very unsettled lately, what with his exams and everything. I know he'd like to see you.

Karen   It's just that I'm working on an extra shift . . .

Sally   But you were on extra shifts all last week!

Karen   I know . . .

Sally   It's terrible the way they make you work there. Honestly, the NHS! It makes you sick . . .

AN OLD LADY TOTTERS PAST *Karen*. THERE IS A LOT OF NOISE IN THE CORRIDOR.

Karen   Look, mum. I can't talk . . .

Sally   I know, dear. Look – I've got to go into town at lunch-time. Shall I pop in for coffee?

Karen   Mum . . .

Sally   It would be nice to see you. Just the two of us.

Karen   Alright . . .

Sally   Come by at one. OK?

THIS IS THE LAST THING THAT *Karen* WANTS.

Karen   OK, mum.

Karen HANGS UP. THEN SIGHS.

BACK IN THE KITCHEN, *Sally* PUTS THE PHONE DOWN AND BEGINS MAKING HER CAKE, SMILING HAPPILY AND HUMMING THE TUNE FROM THE RADIO AD.

CUT TO:

SCENE TEN

Int. Mike's school 11.00 a.m.

IN THE CORRIDOR, *Mike* PASSES A CAREERS NOTICEBOARD WITH ADVICE AND A FEW JOBS PINNED IN PLACE. ALMOST CARELESSLY, HIS EYES FALL ON ONE OF THE JOBS. HE UNPINS IT AND WALKS WITH IT ACROSS THE CORRIDOR. WE SEE A DOOR: 'MR GREEN – CAREERS ADVISOR'.

Mike GOES IN.

CUT TO:

SCENE ELEVEN ▦▦▦▦▦▦▦▦▦▦▦▦▦▦▦▦▦▦▦▦▦▦▦▦▦▦
Int. Mike's school 11.05 a.m.

Sam Green IS THE ONLY ADVISOR ON DUTY. HE IS A
TEACHER WITH SPECIAL RESPONSIBILITIES FOR CAREERS.
YOUNG, TIRED AND BEDRAGGLED, HE'S FED UP WITH A JOB
THAT SEEMS TO OFFER NO REWARDS. AS *Mike* COMES IN, HE
IS TALKING TO A VERY GRAVE FOURTEEN-YEAR-OLD *Boy*.

Green   So you want to be ... an astronaut?

THE FOURTEEN-YEAR-OLD *Boy* NODS HIS HEAD GRAVELY.

Green   Yes, I see. But maybe you should be considering a second
option.   [PAUSE]   How about catering?

CUT TO: ANOTHER ANGLE. *Mike* GOES FURTHER INTO
THE ROOM, GLANCING AT THE VARIOUS POSTERS AND
BOOKS. *Green* CONCLUDES HIS INTERVIEW WITH THE *Boy* BY
HANDING HIM A SHEAF OF LEAFLETS ABOUT CATERING.

Green   Have a look at these. Then come back and we'll talk
again.

THE *Boy* LEAVES WITH THE LEAFLETS. *Green* WAVES *Mike*
TO THE EMPTY CHAIR.

Green   Take a seat, Mike.

Mike SITS DOWN.

Green   How are you?

Mike   OK.

Green   So what can I do for you?

Mike GIVES *Green* THE CARD.

Mike   I want to apply for this.

Green   Garage mechanic? Since when were you interested in
cars?

Mike SHRUGS. *Green* EXAMINES THE CARD.

Green This is three days old. The job's probably gone by now.
Is it what you want?

Mike Yeah ...

Green You sound really enthusiastic, Mike. You're going to
knock them out at the interview, you know that?

Mike Look ...

Green No – you look. You haven't done any of the work in the
tutorial programmes. You've skived off half the time. And
now you come in with this. I mean, you've left it a bit late,
haven't you?

Mike I didn't know what I wanted.

Green And you do now?

Mike I know what I don't want.

Green Yeah?

Mike A job making dollies.

CUT TO: ANOTHER ANGLE. *Green* TAKES A PACKET OF
CIGARETTES OUT OF HIS DESK.

Green You want a cigarette?

Mike I'm not meant to smoke in school.

Green They're chocolate cigarettes.

HE TAKES ONE AND CHEWS IT.

Green You know, you really worry me, Mike.

Mike Me?

Green Look – I've got two hundred and twenty kids leaving
school this term. Maybe a dozen of them into full-time
employment. You don't need me to tell you that it's a
nasty world out there. Everyone wants a slice of the cake
but suddenly there isn't enough to go round. Right?

Mike What are you ...?

Green I'm trying to tell you that if you're going to get anywhere,
you've got to know what you want and then get out there
and fight for it. But look at you – slouching there. After a
job three days too late ... a job you don't even want. It's a
buyers' market out there, Mike.

Mike	A market? That makes us sound like cattle.
Green	That's not what I'm saying.
Mike	Isn't it? But that *is* all we are, isn't it?
Green	Not if you put your mind to it.
Mike	Put my mind to what? There aren't any jobs, anyway.
Green	There are training courses. YTS and further education. But that's not the point. Jobs aren't everything. There's more to life than the work you do.
Mike	Oh, that's great – coming from a careers advisor.
Green	You want a career, I'll advise you. But I don't think that's why you're here, Mike. You're not looking for a job. You're looking for yourself.
Mike	Very deep, Mr Green. I'll think about that one while I'm waiting for my dole.

Mike EXITS ANGRILY.

CUT TO:

SCENE TWELVE

Int. Mike's school 11.30 a.m.

Mike PAUSES IN THE CORRIDOR. PART OF HIS CONVERSATION WITH *Green* ECHOES IN HIS HEAD.

| Green | [v/o] It's a buyers' market out there, Mike. |
| Mike | [v/o] A market? That makes us sound like cattle. |

Mike MOVES AWAY. HE PASSES THE OPEN DOOR OF A CLASSROOM. THE CAMERA STAYS ON THE DOOR, THEN ENTERS.

CUT TO:

SCENE THIRTEEN

Int. Mike's school (classroom) 11.40 a.m.

Steve IS STANDING IN FRONT OF A BLACKBOARD, ON WHICH IS WRITTEN A QUOTE FROM GEORGE ORWELL – 'ALL ANIMALS ARE EQUAL' – THE CLASS (MIXED AND MULTI-RACIAL) IS LISTENING TO HIM WHILE HE READS A PASSAGE FROM *Animal Farm*.

Steve   [READING] Let us face it: our lives are miserable, laborious and short. We are born, we are given just so much food as will keep the breath in our bodies; and the very instant that our usefulness has come to an end we are slaughtered with hideous cruelty . . .

FADE TO:

SCENE   FOURTEEN

Ext. An office block Day

ESTABLISHING SHOT: IT COULD BE ANY OFFICE, ANYWHERE. THE CAMERA CLOSES IN.

Steve   [v/o] No animal in England knows the meaning of happiness or leisure after he is a year old.

FADE TO:

SCENE   FIFTEEN

Int. The office block Day

THE CAMERA FOLLOWS A NERVOUS *Pearson* AS HE WALKS DOWN AN ENDLESS, DEEPLY CARPETED CORRIDOR TOWARDS A SET OF DOUBLE DOORS.

Steve   [v/o] No animal in England is free. The life of an animal is misery and slavery: that is the plain truth.

FADE TO:

SCENE   SIXTEEN

Int. Conference room in office 12.00 midday

Steve's VOICE FADES OUT AS WE ENTER THE VAST,

OPPRESSIVE ROOM WITH *Pearson*. THE ROOM IS FURNISHED WITH A LONG WOODEN TABLE, SURROUNDED BY CHAIRS. BUT THERE IS NOBODY IN THE ROOM. *Pearson* WAITS BY THE CHAIR AT ONE END OF THE TABLE. A TV STANDS AT THE FAR END, IN THE POSITION OF THE *Chairman*. AND IT IS ON THE TV THAT THE (AMERICAN) *Chairman* APPEARS, HE APPEARS ALMOST COMPLETELY DEHUMANIZED IN THE TECHNI-CALITIES OF THIS BIZARRE SATELLITE CONFERENCE.

Chairman   Please sit down, Mr Pearson.

Pearson   [NERVOUS] Thank you, sir.

Pearson SITS DOWN SO THAT HE NOW FACES THE TV SCREEN.

Chairman   I understand you're the Personnel Manager of QT-Pie Dolls.

Pearson   Yes, sir.

Chairman   And you know we have now purchased the company as an ongoing concern?

Pearson   I don't have all the details, sir.

Chairman   Relocation to Scotland with a statutory grant of £2.7 million. New plant. A workforce effectively halved. Wages rates down fifteen to twenty per cent. And total clearance from your Department of Industry. What do you think?

Pearson COUGHS NERVOUSLY.

Pearson   I think some of the workers, sir, may ...

Chairman   That's why you're here, Pearson. Are we going to have problems? And how bad will the problems be?

Pearson   Well ... there's hardly any union involvement. But I don't think anyone will take it lying down.

Chairman   I know. But we don't want a Wapping on our hands, Pearson. It's bad for business. Bad for the company image.

Pearson   There may still be resistance.

Chairman   I want that checked, Pearson. That's your job. Pull out the ring-leaders and get rid of them. Do you read me?

Pearson   [AGHAST] Yes ...

Chairman	You and your family will be coming with the firm to Glasgow?
Pearson	Yes, sir.
Chairman	Good. You know the men. You make sure this thing goes through. [A PAUSE] I'd hate to see you miss that train ...

CUT TO: REACTION ON *Pearson*. HE SWALLOWS NERVOUSLY AND SWEATS.

CUT TO:

SCENE   SEVENTEEN   ▦▦▦▦▦▦▦▦▦▦▦▦▦▦▦▦▦▦

Ext. Hospital 1.15 p.m.

ESTABLISHING SHOT: *Karen's* HOSPITAL – A TYPICAL NHS BUILDING. SOME PARTS BRAND NEW. SOME PARTS OLD AND UGLY.

CUT TO:

SCENE   EIGHTEEN   ▦▦▦▦▦▦▦▦▦▦▦▦▦▦▦▦▦▦

Int. Hospital (cafeteria) 1.15 p.m.

Karen AND *Sally* ARE HAVING COFFEE TOGETHER.

Sally	This new boyfriend of yours – you haven't told me anything about him.
Karen	You'll meet him this evening.
Sally	So you're both coming.
Karen	I said I would.
Sally	I know you think I'm silly, but it's important to me ... the family. You and Mike and Steve ...
Karen	I never said you were silly.
Sally	Look at the world today. Everywhere you look, it's just problems. Unemployment and racism and sexism and all those other isms. But if you can be close as a family,

somehow they don't matter so much.

Karen   Oh, mum ...

Sally   There you go again. But if you'd only settle down and get married yourself, you'd see what I mean. There's nothing certain in life. But at least you know where you are when you're with your family.

CUT TO:

SCENE NINETEEN

Ext. QT-Pie Dolls Ltd (car park) 5.00 p.m.

TOWARDS THE END OF THE DAY. *John* HAS JUST HEARD THE NEWS ABOUT THE AMERICAN PURCHASE OF HIS FACTORY. HE IS SHELL-SHOCKED. *Pearson* GOES PAST HIM. THE TWO LOOK AT EACH OTHER. *John* IS ACCUSING.

CUT TO:

SCENE TWENTY

Ext. Steve's school 9.00 a.m.

Steve HAS JUST ARRIVED AT SCHOOL. HE IS WALKING DOWN A STRETCH OF THE PLAYGROUND THAT IS FAIRLY ISOLATED – POSSIBLY BEHIND THE BICYCLE SHED. AS USUAL, HE IS FAIRLY NERVOUS. *Steve* IS ONE OF LIFE'S VICTIMS – AND KNOWS IT. *Sonia*, A LITTLE OLDER THAN HIM (FIFTEEN), SUDDENLY APPEARS OUT OF NOWHERE AND STOPS HIM.

Sonia   Hello, Steve.

Steve   Sonia?

Sonia   Where are you going?

Steve   Registration.

Sonia GLANCES AT HIS BAG.

Sonia   I hear you're into ice-skating. You got your skates in there?

Steve   [GUARDED] Yes.

Sonia	How about trousers – with sequins on?
Steve	I don't wear them!
Sonia	Torville does. Or is it Dean? I can never remember which one's the man.
Steve	Chris Dean. And Jayne Torville.
Sonia	I think it's really great – ice-skating. Are you going to do it – you know – professional, like?

Steve ISN'T SURE WHAT'S GOING ON. *Sonia* SEEMS FRIENDLY, FLATTERING. BUT HE'S NOT CONVINCED.

Steve	I could . . .
Sonia	Could I come and watch some time?
Steve	I don't know.

Steve TRIES TO WALK PAST, BUT *Sonia* STOPS HIM.

Sonia	You know, I really fancy you, Steve. Honest. You've got a lovely bum.
Steve	Sonia . . .
Sonia	What's wrong? Don't you like girls or something? You haven't got a girl-friend.
Steve	Well . . .

SHY AND EMBARRASSED, *Steve* IS NONETHELESS BEGINNING TO COME ROUND.

Sonia	You could go out with me, if you liked.
Steve	What about you and Derek?
Sonia	We've split up. How about the disco? Down at the youth club?
Steve	Well . . . all right . . .
Sonia	That's all right, then.

SHE SMILES SWEETLY AT HIM.

| Sonia | Aren't you going to give me a kiss, then? If we're going out . . . |

Steve HESITATES. BUT IT WOULD SEEM CHURLISH TO REFUSE. HE KISSES HER LIGHTLY ON THE CHEEK. THE NEXT MOMENT THE ILLUSION IS SHATTERED AS SHE STEPS BACK

WITH A CRY OF REVULSION, RUBBING AT HER CHEEK.

Sonia   Oh, shit! AIDS!

CUT TO: ANOTHER ANGLE. A WHOLE BUNCH OF KIDS (BLACK AND WHITE, MALE AND FEMALE) COME LEAPING OUT OF THEIR HIDING PLACE. THEY FALL ONTO *Steve* PULLING HIM AWAY FROM THE REVOLTED *Sonia* AND SENDING HIM FLYING ONTO THE GROUND. THEY SHOUT AT THE SAME TIME:

First kid   What are you doing, Steve!

Second kid   He's got AIDS!

Third kid   Get the queer!

Fourth kid   Don't touch him!

Teacher   [v/o] What's going on here?

CUT TO: ANOTHER ANGLE. A *Teacher* HAS APPEARED AS IF FROM NOWHERE, WALKING TO HIS OFFICE WHICH HAPPENS TO BE NEARBY. AS HE APPROACHES, *Sonia* AND THE OTHER KIDS SCATTER AND RUN, LEAVING *Steve* ON THE GROUND. HE HAS BEEN HURT IN THE FRACAS. HIS TROUSERS ARE TORN, HIGH UP ON HIS THIGH, AND THE SKIN IS GASHED. THE *Teacher* STANDS OVER HIM.

SCENE   TWENTY-ONE

Int. Mike's school 11.30 a.m.

Mike HESITATES IN FRONT OF A PUBLIC TELEPHONE. HE IS STILL HOLDING THE JOB NOTICE THAT HE TOOK DOWN FROM THE BOARD. SHOULD HE RING? HE DECIDES. HE GOES INTO THE PHONE BOX AND DIALS A NUMBER.

CUT TO:

SCENE   TWENTY-TWO

Int. Williams' home (dining room) 4.00 p.m.

CLOSE SHOT: ON THE FINISHED BIRTHDAY CAKE,

COMPLETE WITH SIXTEEN CANDLES. END MUSIC TRACK.

CUT TO: WIDER ANGLE. *Steve* AND *Mike* ARE AT THE
TABLE. BOTH HAVE HAD A BAD DAY. *Sally* LOOKS AT THEM
ANXIOUSLY AS SHE ARRANGES THE REST OF THE FOOD.

Sally	So how was your day, Stephen?
Steve	It was OK.
Sally	How about that essay of yours. On *Animal Farm*. Did you get a good mark?
Steve	Yeah.
Sally	Well, you could sound more pleased about it.

SHE LOOKS AT HER WATCH.

Sally	I don't know where your father is. It's not like him to be late.

PAUSE.

Sally	We can start without him, if you like.
Mike	Not hungry.
Sally	Oh, Mikey! After all the work I've gone to. Are you going out with Sharon later?
Mike	I might be.
Sally	Saving your appetite, I suppose.

A CAR PULLS UP IN THE DRIVE OUTSIDE.

Steve	Here's dad.
Sally	Good. Come on, Mike. You could manage a smile. It's not every day you're sixteen.
Mike	Approximately.
Sally	What?
Mike	Approximately sixteen.

Sally DOESN'T WANT TO GET INVOLVED IN *THAT*
DISCUSSION. SHE GRABS A PLATE OF SAUSAGE ROLLS AND
OFFERS ONE TO *Steve*.

Sally	Have a sausage roll, dear. You might as well tuck in.
Steve	Thanks.

Steve TAKES THE SAUSAGE ROLL ... BUT HE DOESN'T EAT IT.

CUT TO: ANOTHER ANGLE. THE DOOR OPENS AND *John* COMES IN. HE IS SLIGHTLY DRUNK.

Sally   Darling! Where have you been? We were about to start without you.

John   Start without me.

Sally   You've been drinking!

John GROPES FOR A CHAIR.

John   [TO *Mike*] You can forget that job at the factory, Mike. You didn't want it. You wanted to be free to choose. Well, you *are* free. They're shutting it down.

Sally   What?

John SITS DOWN HEAVILY.

John   It's been sold to an American company and they're going to move. To Scotland.

Sally   They can't do that!

John   They can do anything they like.

Steve   What'll happen to you, dad?

John   Oh – they'll pay me off, won't they? But how long do you think that'll last? We've got the mortgage, the HP ... we're up to our ears in credit. The car'll go, of course. And what sort of future do you think there is for me? I'm forty-seven. What sort of choice do you think there is for me?

CUT TO: ANOTHER ANGLE. *Mike* GETS UP.

Sally   Mike! Where are you going?

Mike   Well, there's no point in sitting here, is there?

John   Oh, that's nice, that is. Rats desert the sinking ship.

Sally   [TO JOHN] Not on his birthday! Honestly! We're a family! We can face up to this together.   [TO *Steve*]   Light the cake, Steve.

CUT TO: ANGLE FAVOURING *Steve*. HE IS PARALYSED – UNABLE TO COPE – UNABLE TO DO ANYTHING.

CUT TO: ANGLE FAVOURING *John*. HE GETS UP AND GOES OVER TO THE SIDEBOARD.

John I need a drink.

Mike And for me.

John You're too young.

Mike Oh, yeah? I was a man this morning, wasn't I? A wage earner?

Mike TAKES OUT A PACKET OF CIGARETTES. HE HAS NEVER SMOKED BEFORE. HE'S ABOUT TO LIGHT ONE, BUT *John* STOPS HIM, GRABBING THE HAND WITH THE MATCH. THE MATCH IS DROPPED INTO THE DUSTBIN.

Mike And I'm allowed to smoke. That's the law.

John Not in this house, it isn't!

Sally You've never smoked!

John HAS TAKEN OUT A BOTTLE OF SCOTCH. *Sally* IS TORN BETWEEN THE THREE OF THEM. THE DRUNK HUSBAND, THE PARALYSED *Steve*, THE SURLY *Mike*. TO ADD TO THE TROUBLES, THE WASTEPAPER BASKET IS NOW ON FIRE. SMOKE BILLOWS OUT.

Steve Mum ...

Sally Not now, dear.

Steve Mum!

Steve HAS SEEN THE DUSTBIN. AND NOW, *Sally* SEES IT, TOO.

Sally Oh my God! Mike! What have you done?

John Here.

John POURS HIS WHISKY ONTO THE BIN.

Sally Not whisky!

FLAMES EXPLODE OUT OF THE METAL BIN.

Sally John!

Mike LAUGHS.

Sally It's not funny, Michael! Do something!

Mike Right!

Mike GRABS A WET TEA TOWEL FROM THE SINK AND STUFFS IT INTO THE BIN. BUT SMOKE SEEPS OUT FROM BENEATH THE MATERIAL. *Sally* LOOKS ABOUT HER IN BEWILDERMENT.

Sally   I don't understand! What's happening to us? What's happening to us?

John   Well, don't worry, love. It can't get any worse.

CUT TO: ANOTHER ANGLE. THE DOOR OPENS AND *Karen* (OUT OF UNIFORM) COMES IN. SHE IS HOLDING A GIFT-WRAPPED PARCEL.

Karen   Hello, mum. Hi, dad.

A YOUNG MAN STEPS INTO THE ROOM BEHIND HER. HE IS IN HIS TWENTIES. SMOOTH, WELL-DRESSED. HE IS AN INDIAN.

Karen   This is Sanjay.

CUT TO: REACTION ON *John*. HE DOESN'T NEED TO SAY ANYTHING. WE SUSPECT THE FACT THAT *Sanjay* IS ASIAN DOESN'T HELP, BUT THAT'S NOT THE POINT. THIS IS SIMPLY THE WRONG TIME TO BE MEETING HIS DAUGHTER'S BOYFRIEND ... WITH HIS HOUSE AND FAMILY IN CHAOS.

CUT TO: REACTION ON *Steve* AND *Mike*. THEY CAN'T BELIEVE THE BOMBSHELL THAT HAS JUST HIT THEM.

CUT TO: REACTION ON *Karen*. SHE KNEW IT WASN'T GOING TO BE EASY. BEHIND HER, *Sanjay* WAITS WITH AN EXPRESSION OF POLITE DISMAY.

CUT TO: ANGLE FAVOURING *Sally*. SHE IS SURROUNDED BY THE SHATTERED REMNANTS OF HER FAMILY, BUT SHE IS DETERMINED TO SAVE THE DAY. DESPERATELY, SHE LOOKS ABOUT HER. WHAT CAN SHE SAY?

Sally   Karen ... Sanjay ...

CUT TO: ANGLE FAVOURING *Sanjay*. IT IS LEFT TO COOL, CALM *Sanjay* TO SAVE THE DAY.

Sanjay   Good evening, Mrs Williams.

HE SEES THE CAKE.

Sanjay   Do you think I could have a piece of cake?

CUT TO: BLACK OUT.

CUT TO: END CREDITS.

It's Never Black and White

CHARACTERS

Mike Williams

Leo Young

Ian McClintock

Frances Young

Mr Sloane

Magistrate

Actor/Poet

Barman

SCENE ONE ▦▦▦▦▦▦▦▦▦▦▦▦▦▦▦▦▦▦

Int. Courtroom 11.30 a.m.

> THE MAGISTRATE IS CROSS-EXAMINING *Mike* – THE SCENE BEING THE SAME AS IN *A Piece of the Cake.* BUT THIS TIME THE ONLY RECOGNISABLE CHARACTERS IN THE COURTROOM ARE *Mike, McClintock* AND THE *Magistrate.* ONCE AGAIN, *Mike* SEEMS LOST IN THE (ALMOST SURREALIST) SHADOWS OF THE GREAT ROOM.

Magistrate Why did you leave your job?

Mike It wasn't a job. It was a training scheme.

Magistrate Your training scheme, then.

Mike I didn't leave. I was thrown out.

Magistrate Why?

Mike I was caught nicking a spark plug.

> CUT TO: ANOTHER ANGLE. *McClintock*, THE GARAGE OWNER, LISTENS TO THIS WITH A CERTAIN DEGREE OF SMUGNESS.

Magistrate [v/o] Did you take it?

Mike [v/o] Yes.

> CUT TO: RESUME ON *Mike*.

Magistrate Is that why you later returned and vandalised the garage where you worked?

> CUT TO:

SCENE TWO ▦▦▦▦▦▦▦▦▦▦▦▦▦▦▦▦▦▦

First insert

> IN BLACK AND WHITE. NIGHT. A STREET. IN SLOW MOTION, *Mike* THROWS A BRICK AT AN UNIDENTIFIED TARGET.

> CUT TO:

SCENE THREE ▦▦▦▦▦▦▦▦▦▦▦▦▦▦▦▦▦

Int. Courtroom 11.00 a.m.

Mike No! But it's too difficult to explain.

HE GESTURES TO *McClintock.*

Mike He called me a thief.

Magistrate But you were a thief. By your own admission.

Mike It was just a spark plug. It wasn't even worth a quid.

CUT TO: ANOTHER ANGLE FAVOURING *Mike.*

Mike My dad – before his factory got shut down – my dad always came home with pens and screwdrivers and that sort of thing. But it was all right for him. Nobody ever accused him of anything. So why me?

Magistrate But the spark plug was what started it all, wasn't it? That's when things began to go wrong for you.

Mike I wasn't a thief. You can *call* me that. My dad called me that. But it's never black and white, is it? Everyone wants it to be. The system. But it isn't as easy as that. Inside, it's different. It isn't black and white . . .

CUT TO:

SCENE FOUR ▦▦▦▦▦▦▦▦▦▦▦▦▦▦▦▦▦

OPENING CREDITS (THE SAME AS IN *A Piece of the Cake*).

CUT TO:

SCENE FIVE ▦▦▦▦▦▦▦▦▦▦▦▦▦▦▦▦▦

Ext. McClintock's garage 11.30 a.m.

ESTABLISHING SHOT: A SMALL GARAGE, PROBABLY AT THE QUIET END OF A HIGH STREET. THIS IS A RESPECTABLE, FAMILY-RUN BUSINESS. IT SPECIALISES IN MOTS AND

EXHAUST REPLACEMENTS.

CUT TO:

SCENE SIX

Int. McClintock's office 11.30 a.m.

A SMALL, UNTIDY OFFICE, PRESIDED OVER BY *McClintock*, A MAN IN THE ARTHUR DALEY MOULD, BUT GENERALLY MORE HONEST AND MORE SUCCESSFUL. THIS IS HIS BUSINESS, BUILT WITH HIS OWN TWO HANDS, AND HE LIKES PEOPLE TO KNOW IT.

OPPOSITE HIM, AND SMARTLY DRESSED FOR THE INTERVIEW, SITS *Leo Young*, EIGHTEEN YEARS OLD, INTELLIGENT, PERSONABLE – AND BLACK. HE HAS BEEN UNEMPLOYED FOR FIVE MONTHS.

THIS IS A FRIENDLY, RELAXED INTERVIEW. THERE IS NO HINT OF RACISM IN THE PROCEEDINGS UNTIL, PERHAPS, RIGHT AT THE END.

McClintock   Aye, you're right, it needs a new ignition coil. But can you fit it in?

Leo   No sweat.

McClintock   And tell me now. If I asked you to work on a McPherson strut, would you know what I'd be talking about?

Leo   It's a sort of suspension, isn't it?

McClintock   So it is. How about a drum brake assembly?

Leo   No sweat.

McClintock   You don't sweat a lot, do you, Mr Young? Describe one for me.

Leo   Two brake shoes. Mounted on a back-plate. Inside a drum.

McClintock IS CLEARLY IMPRESSED.

McClintock   You know your cars. Do you have one of your own?

Leo   No. A bike. An old BMW.

McClintock   And how long did you say you'd been out of work?

Leo	Five months, Mr McClintock.
McClintock	That's a lot of time to be wasting. [WITH A SMILE] But I suppose you people just hang out and enjoy yourselves, eh?
Leo	'Us people', Mr McClintock?
McClintock	Kids. Teenagers. Och – I was one once. But then again. I was never out of work.

McClintock REFERS TO *Leo's* CV, WHICH IS ON THE DESK IN FRONT OF HIM.

McClintock	I see you've had a bit of trouble in the past.
Leo	I was young then.
McClintock	You're young now, laddy. You had a bad school record.
Leo	It was a bad school.
McClintock	Was it now?
Leo	I didn't like it.
McClintock	You didn't like your last job very much, either. You left it pretty snappy.
Leo	I didn't get on with the boss.
McClintock	And what makes you think you'll get on with me?
Leo	Well ... I'm not anti-Scottish, if that's what you mean.

McClintock ACKNOWLEDGES THIS HALF-JOKE WITH A HALF-SMILE.

McClintock	Aye, well. I'll let you know in due course, Mr Young. A couple of days. No sweat?

Leo IS DISAPPOINTED. HE IGNORES THE SLIGHT BARB AT THE END OF *McClintock's* LAST SENTENCE.

Leo	Oh. I hoped you'd be able to tell me right away, Mr McClintock
McClintock	And why did you think that?
Leo	Well ... it's not as if the job has been advertised or anything.
McClintock	True. But it will be. We've got to be fair, haven't we?
Leo	Well ...

McClintock	I'll be seeing a few other people in the next couple o' days.
Leo	But you said I had the right experience.
McClintock	I'll be the judge of that, laddy. It's not just a question of experience ...
Leo	What else, Mr McClintock?
McClintock	Attitude, for one. Don't you worry, I'll be in touch.

Leo WANTS TO ARGUE, BUT HE REALISES IT WILL ONLY DAMAGE HIS CAUSE. HE GETS UP TO LEAVE.

| Leo | Thank you, Mr McClintock. |

Leo MAKES FOR THE DOOR. BUT BEFORE HE GOES, *McClintock* HAS ONE MORE QUESTION.

| McClintock | One last question, Mr Young. The two cylinders in a hydraulic system. What are they called? |

Leo CONSIDERS, BUT THE QUESTION HAS COME OUT OF THE BLUE. HE FALTERS.

| Leo | I'm afraid you've got me there, Mr McClintock. |

McClintock SMILES AT A PRIVATE (RACIST) JOKE.

| McClintock | I'm surprised. You ought to know that one. One is called the master   [PAUSE]   And the other one's the slave. |

CUT TO:

SCENE SEVEN

Int. Garage 12.00 midday

Leo LEAVES THE GARAGE, MAKING HIS WAY PAST A NUMBER OF WORKERS, BUSY SERVICING THE USUAL ASSORTMENT OF CARS. IN THE BACKGROUND, *Mike* SEES HIM AND LOOKS UP, QUESTIONINGLY. *Leo* TURNS A SURREPTITIOUS THUMB DOWN AND WALKS OUT.

CUT TO:

SCENE EIGHT ▨▨▨▨▨▨▨▨▨▨▨▨▨▨▨▨▨▨▨▨▨▨▨

Ext. A block of flats 1.00 p.m.

> *Leo* GETS OFF HIS ANCIENT MOTORBIKE OUTSIDE A BLOCK
> OF FLATS. NOT ONE OF THE FAMOUS EYESORES, BUT
> CERTAINLY NOT THE MOST PREPOSSESSING OF PLACES,
> EITHER. WE HEAR THE BEGINNING OF A CONVERSATION AS
> HE ARRIVES.

Mike	[V/O] Mr McClintock – could I have a word?
McClintock	[V/O] Michael? Come in, lad.

CUT TO:

SCENE NINE ▨▨▨▨▨▨▨▨▨▨▨▨▨▨▨▨▨▨▨▨▨▨▨

Int. McClintock's office 1.00 p.m.

> *Mike* SITS DOWN OPPOSITE *McClintock*. THE ATMOSPHERE
> IS UNCOMFORTABLE AND WILL RAPIDLY BECOME WORSE.

Mike	I was wondering about Leo.
McClintock	Young? Ah – so it was you who put him up, was it?
Mike	He's a mate.
McClintock	Is he now? A 'mate' ...
Mike	I just thought he'd be right. I mean, there's nothing about cars he doesn't know.
McClintock	Aye, I'll give you that. But there are other considerations.
Mike	Like what? He's a great mechanic. He's dead straight. He's a hard worker. And he needs the job.
McClintock	So do two and a half million other people, laddie.
Mike	But what's wrong with Leo? I mean, I'd have thought he was perfect ...

CUT TO:

SCENE TEN ▦▦▦▦▦▦▦▦▦▦▦▦▦▦▦▦▦▦
Int. Leo's flat 3.00 p.m.

Leo LIVES WITH HIS MOTHER. THE INTERIOR IS
COMFORTABLE AND TASTEFULLY DECORATED. *Frances
Young* IS AN ARTIST. HER WORK IS IN PLENTIFUL EVIDENCE –
AS ARE THE AFRICAN ARTEFACTS THAT MAY HAVE INSPIRED
IT. THIS IS A STRONG, POLITICALLY ACTIVE AND WELL-
INFORMED WOMAN. HER ONE WEAKNESS? IN HER DEVOTION
TO HER WORK SHE HAS LITTLE TIME FOR HER SON.

AS *Leo* ENTERS (INTRODUCED BY *McClintock's* VOICE-OVER),
SHE IS FINISHING A SKETCH. THE DIALOGUE THAT
FOLLOWS MAKES NO ATTEMPT TO IMITATE ANY FORM OF
PATOIS. IT PROVIDES A STRUCTURE AROUND WHICH THE
ACTORS CAN IMPROVISE.

McClintock [V/O] What's wrong with Leo?

Frances So how did it go?

Leo It didn't. It was a no-go.

Frances They didn't give you the job?

Leo They didn't say.

Frances Then how do you know?

Leo Because they said it without saying it.

A PAUSE. *Leo* SLUMPS INTO A CHAIR.

Frances You want some tea? It's in the kitchen.

Leo I'm not hungry. What's that?

Frances A sketch. 'Socrates in Africa'.

Leo Who's Socrates?

Frances He was a philosopher.

Leo Oh. White?

Frances Yes, he was white.

Leo He could have been a garage mechanic, then.

ANOTHER PAUSE. *Frances* PUTS DOWN HER SKETCH,
EXASPERATED.

Frances	Leo – you want to moan, you go find someone else to listen. I'm busy, OK?
Leo	Yeah. You're always busy.
Frances	There's something wrong with that?
Leo	Mum – I've been five months now looking for work. Five months!
Frances	And how long did you hold on to your last job for, Leo? Five weeks ...
Leo	That wasn't my fault.
Frances	It never is, is it?

Frances REALISES SHE ISN'T GOING TO BE ABLE TO GO ON WITH HER WORK. SHE THROWS THE SKETCH PAD DOWN.

Frances	All right, let's hear it, then.

CUT TO:

SCENE ELEVEN ▨▨▨▨▨▨▨▨▨▨▨▨▨▨▨▨▨▨▨▨▨▨

Int. McClintock's office 3.15 p.m.

AS BEFORE. *Frances* PROVIDES THE VOICE-OVER INTRODUCTION, AS WE REJOIN THE SCENE.

Frances	[v/o] The all-purpose excuse ...
McClintock	He's black.

Mike IS STARTLED BY THE BLUNTNESS OF THIS COMMENT.

McClintock	Aye – I've surprised you, haven't I? It's not the sort of thing you're supposed to say.
Mike	But what difference does it make?
McClintock	I don't like black people. I don't trust them.
Mike	But that's crazy, Mr McClintock. I mean, you don't even *know* Leo.
McClintock	I don't want to know him – or his sort. This is my business. I built it up with my own hands. I hire who I want to hire. Are you with me? You may not like my views, but I've a right to them. The same as anybody else.

Mike   But you're not even thinking . . .

BEFORE *Mike* CAN CONTINUE, *McClintock* CUTS IN.

McClintock   I'll tell you this much, Michael. They're their own worst enemy. Out there on the street with their drugs and their music, keeping themselves to themselves . . . they don't want to know us. They hate us! Aye, you can talk about 'racial prejudice'. But they're as prejudiced as anyone. They hate us, but they still expect everything to be handed to them on a plate.

CUT TO:

SCENE TWELVE

Int. Leo's flat 3.15 p.m.

McClintock   [V/O] And why? Just one reason.

Leo   . . . because I'm black.

Frances   [SURPRISED] Are you? Son – you never told me . . .

Leo   Mum . . .

Frances   Why do you always have to say the word like an insult, Leo?

Leo   Because in this country, it is an insult.

Frances   No. 'Nigger' is an insult. 'Wog' is an insult. But you never even think what black really means.

Leo   I don't think it. I live it.

Frances   Do you? Have I seen you outside Sainsbury's, picketing them for their South African imports? Have I seen you on a demo to get Nelson Mandela out of jail? How long has he been there? Do you know? Have you read Martin Luther King? Get a map. Can you even point to Botswana without looking for the name?

Leo   That's got nothing to do with it . . .

Frances   How can you be strong without your roots? Look at the Asians. And the Jews.

Leo   The Jews are white.

Frances And it didn't help them an awful lot back in 1935, did it?

A PAUSE. THEN, MORE GENTLY ...

Frances Leo, our names have been taken from us. Our religion and our language. But we're still black. And we don't need to be ashamed of it ...

SHE PICKS UP THE SKETCH.

Frances Socrates went to Africa. That was where western philosophy began. With us. We were creating art and music while the English were still painting themselves blue and hiding in the trees.

Leo Maybe I should have told Mr McClintock that.

CUT TO:

SCENE THIRTEEN

Int. McClintock's office 3.30 p.m.

Frances [V/O SCORNFUL] And what's your Mr McClintock?

Mike You're a racist!

McClintock I don't want your lip, son.

A PAUSE. *McClintock* DECIDES NOT TO LOSE HIS TEMPER. HE'S TOO SELF-ASSURED FOR THAT.

McClintock Racist. Racism. What are they? Just words, used by social workers and left-wing politicians with an axe to grind. Suppose I am a racist? What's so wrong with it? Is it really something to be ashamed of?

Mike I don't believe what I'm hearing. You can't mean that.

McClintock Why not?

Mike It's not black people who are screwing up this country. It's racists. People like you.

McClintock I warn you, son. You're skating on thin ice.

Mike I'm not breaking any law – you are. What you've just said. It's against the law.

McClintock   And you think laws can affect the way people think? Oh – they can try. I've had people round from the council before and I dare say I'll have 'em again. But d'you know something, laddie? We Scots are a stubborn lot. And the more laws there are, the more self-righteous bleeding hearts there are, the more we'll dig our feet in. You can say what you like, but that's human nature. And it won't change.

CUT TO:

SCENE FOURTEEN

Second insert

A STREET. NIGHT. ANOTHER ANGLE, AS *Mike* THROWS A BRICK. THIS TIME WE SEE IT ACTUALLY LEAVE HIS HANDS AND START THE JOURNEY THAT IT WILL TAKE THE WHOLE EPISODE TO CONCLUDE. (NOTE: THIS INSERT IS ALSO IN BLACK AND WHITE.)

CUT TO:

SCENE FIFTEEN

Int. Theatre stage 9.00 a.m.

Actor/Poet   You try your best,
You don't succeed,
Try again, get disappointed.
Again and again the same old story.
Who is at fault?
Who is to blame?

CUT TO:

SCENE SIXTEEN ░░░░░░░░░░░░░░░

Ext. Street outside Leo's flat 9.30 a.m.

> *Leo* TRIES TO GET HIS BIKE TO START. IT WON'T. HE LOSES
> HIS TEMPER WITH IT.

Actor/Poet   [v/o] Some people say you're lacking quality,
Then they show that you have.
It's your attitude.
So you take offence.

SCENE SEVENTEEN ░░░░░░░░░░░░░░

Int./Ext. Tube train 10.00 a.m.

> *Leo* TAKES A TUBE, LOST IN THE CROWD.

Actor/Poet   [v/o] You are then rude.
Sometimes they are so blatant, it's crude.

> CUT TO:

SCENE EIGHTEEN ░░░░░░░░░░░░░░░

Int./Ext. Station 10.05 a.m.

> *Leo* PASSES THROUGH THE BARRIER. THE *Guard* WHO
> STAMPS HIS TICKET IS ALSO BLACK.

Actor/Poet   [v/o] Then all the little things in life become
Luxuries.

> CUT TO:

SCENE NINETEEN ░░░░░░░░░░░░░░░

Int. Cafe 10.30 a.m.

> *Leo* IS DRINKING COFFEE WITH A NUMBER OF OTHER BLACK
> KIDS IN A CAFE SUCH AS THE 'CENTREPRISE' IN HACKNEY –
> I.E. A CAFE SPECIALISING IN 'ALTERNATIVE' OR ETHNIC
> GROUPINGS.

Actor/Poet [V/O] Even recreation:
No job, no fun.
Not because you're lazy, or ill-equipped,
Or docile.
But because you're on
The wrong side of their smile.

CUT TO:

SCENE TWENTY ▓▓▓▓▓▓▓▓▓▓▓▓▓▓▓▓▓▓▓▓▓▓▓▓▓

Ext. The street 11.00 a.m.

CLOSE SHOT: A GROUP OF BLACK YOUNGSTERS STANDING
ON A STREET CORNER SHOP AND LOOK AT SOMETHING
WITH SUSPICION.

Actor/Poet [V/O] It's a crime.
It's wicked, so unjust.
To find a job you have to
Crawl, creep and beg,
While they watch you squirm,
Crush your confidence like a worm.

CUT TO: REVERSE ANGLE.

THE OBJECT OF THEIR SUSPICION IS A YOUNG *Policeman*. HE
SEES *Leo's* BIKE, WHICH HAS BEEN LEFT ON A YELLOW LINE.
HE TAKES OUT HIS NOTEBOOK.

Actor/Poet [V/O] Stereotyping a monotrack mind.
Hearing only prejudiced connotations about
Your personality.
A slander on your character,
Without even knowing your name.

CUT TO: ANOTHER ANGLE.

Leo WALKS UP THE STREET AND PASSES THE *Policeman*. HE
SEES THAT THERE'S A TICKET ON HIS BIKE. HE RIPS IT OFF.

Actor/Poet [V/O] All this only makes you toughen skin.
Because in this game,
All play to win.
Some have all the chips,
For others, the chips are always down.

What a long road has many bends.
Every mountain has a descent.
So climb in hope,
For everyone has their day.
It will come.
If it breaks many, it will not break me.
I know how to survive.
I will continue to live with a smile,
Even if life doesn't smile with me.
I am,
I am,
I'm me.

Leo TEARS THE TICKET UP AND SCATTERS IT ON THE
PAVEMENT AS HE WALKS AWAY.

CUT TO:

SCENE TWENTY-ONE

Int. The garage 2.00 p.m.

Mike IS FILLING IN A FORM FOR THE SERVICING OF A CAR.
HE SHOWS IT TO THE *Foreman* WHO NODS AND POINTS AND
SAYS SOMETHING – WE DON'T HEAR WHAT BECAUSE OF THE
NOISE OF THE CARS. *Mike* TAKES THE FORM AND WALKS
OFF. THE *Foreman* SMILES. HE'S SET *Mike* UP.

CUT TO: ANOTHER ANGLE.

Mr Sloane, AN ELDERLY AND DISTINGUISHED GENTLEMAN
IN BLAZER AND OLD SCHOOL TIE, IS CHATTING TO
McClintock.

Sloane	So, how's business?
McClintock	I can't complain.
Sloane	You going away this year?
McClintock	Aye. A couple of weeks in Majorca. You?
Sloane	Cruising in Turkey.
McClintock	[WITH A SNIFF] It's all right for some . . .

Mike INTERRUPTS WITH THE INVOICE.

Mike	It's all ready, Mr Sloane.
McClintock	Thank you, Michael.

Mike GIVES *Sloane* THE FORM.

Sloane	What's this?
Mike	It's the invoice. New ignition coil and brake linings.

Sloane TURNS TO *McClintock* INDIGNANTLY.

McClintock	I'm sorry, Edward.

McClintock TAKES THE INVOICE AND SCREWS IT UP.

McClintock	He's a new boy. On a training scheme. He doesn't know a thing.
Sloane	I'll pick up the car . . .

Sloane MOVES AWAY. *McClintock* TURNS ON *Mike*.

McClintock	Have you gone soft? Mr Sloane is a cash-only customer.
Mike	Why?
McClintock	You ever heard of VAT?
Mike	Yes.
McClintock	OK. No invoice – no VAT. Strewth! Don't they teach you kids anything?

CUT TO: ANOTHER ANGLE. *Sloane* DRIVES OFF IN HIS RATHER BATTERED CAR.

Mike	He shouldn't be driving that car.
McClintock	And why not?
Mike	It's not road-worthy.
McClintock	Of course it's road-worthy, laddy. I MOT'd it myself.

CUT TO:

SCENE TWENTY-TWO

Third insert

> A STREET. NIGHT. ANOTHER ANGLE. THE BRICK HAS NOW
> LEFT *Mike's* HAND AND IS TRAVELLING THROUGH THE
> DARKNESS TOWARDS ITS UNSEEN TARGET. IN BLACK AND
> WHITE.

> CUT TO:

SCENE TWENTY-THREE

Int. A gym 7.00 p.m.

> *Mike* IS LYING ON HIS BACK DOING BENCH PRESSES. *Leo* IS
> LYING ON THE OTHER SIDE OF HIM, HEAD-TO-HEAD, DOING
> THE SAME EXERCISES. THEIR CONVERSATION IS HELD
> BETWEEN GRUNTS.

Mike He's as bent as a six-pound note. Sloane gets his car
fixed and his MOT done. Mr McClintock gets the cash,
that goes right into his back pocket.

Leo Yeah. Well, that doesn't help me none.

Mike They're just a bunch of crooks. Only that's not the way
they see it. Went to the same public school, didn't they?
You scratch my back, I'll scratch yours.

Leo No, thanks.

Mike [FINISHING] I'm done.

Leo How many was that?

Mike Twenty-five.

Leo Like Hell.

Mike Yeah. It was like Hell. You gonna have a shower?

Leo Just ten more . . .

> *Leo* CONTINUES WITH THE WEIGHTS. *Mike* WATCHES HIM IN
> HALF-ADMIRATION.

> CUT TO:

SCENE   TWENTY-FOUR ░░░░░░░░░░░░░░░░░░░░░░░░░░

Int. Gym shower rooms 7.45 p.m.

Mike AND *Leo* ARE IN THE SHOWERS.

Mike	So you heard . . .
Leo	Yeah. And no. No dice.
Mike	McClintock's a bastard.
Leo	Yeah? I quite liked him.
Mike	Get off!
Leo	No, I thought he was OK.
Mike	He didn't give you the job.
Leo	He checked me out. Two years back I got into trouble – you know.
Mike	Yeah. I know.
Leo	Yeah. Well, that's why.
Mike	That's not true.
Leo	I know that. You know that. He knows that. But there's sod all that anyone can do.
Mike	So, what *are* you going to do?
Leo	My old lady wants me to find my roots.
Mike	You what?
Leo	So maybe I'll take up gardening.

CUT TO:

SCENE   TWENTY-FIVE ░░░░░░░░░░░░░░░░░░░░░░░░░░

Int. Private drinking club 10.00 p.m.

McClintock AND *Sloane* ARE DRINKING BITTER IN A QUIET PRIVATE CLUB.

McClintock	Sorry about that business this morning.

Sloane	Don't mention it, McClintock. Actually, there's something I've been meaning to ask you. You met my son, Eric?
McClintock	I don't think I've had the pleasure.
Sloane	Oh, it's no pleasure. He's a long-haired lout. Thick as two planks. The school would've expelled him if I hadn't stumped up the readies for the new swimming-pool. The thing is, he wants to go into the car business when he leaves.
McClintock	And you want me to take him on?
Sloane	Yes. I mean, if you asked him to change a tyre he wouldn't know where to look. But a few months with you ... Of course, if you haven't got a vacancy ...
McClintock	I haven't, but send him over anyway. [SLYLY] I'm sure something can be arranged.

SCENE TWENTY-SIX

Ext. Outside gym 10.10 p.m.

Leo AND *Mike* WALK TOGETHER.

Mike	You know what I get paid on my training scheme? Peanuts. Same as the dole. But you ought to see the hours I put in.
Leo	Well, it's training, isn't it?
Mike	Sure. Training for what?
Leo	Maybe you'll get a job there.
Mike	If I want it. I don't like being exploited. Know what I mean?
Leo	I suppose it depends how you look at it, Mike.
Mike	Oh, sure. That's it, isn't it? Exploitation. Racism. Stealing and cheating. They don't mean anything, do they? It just depends how you *look* at them.

CUT TO: ANOTHER ANGLE. THERE'S A PUB ACROSS THE STREET.

Mike   You want a drink?

SCENE TWENTY-SEVEN ▨▨▨▨▨▨▨▨▨▨▨▨▨▨▨
Int. Pub 10.20 p.m.

    Mike BUYS THE DRINKS AT THE BAR.

Mike   A pint of Guinness, please. And a lemonade.

    HE TURNS SOURLY TO *Leo.*

Mike   You want a cherry in it?

    Leo GRIMACES.

Mike   You really don't drink?

Leo   I don't like the taste.

    THE *Barman* PASSES OVER THE DRINKS. *Mike* THROWS DOWN A COUPLE OF ONE-POUND COINS.

Leo   I see you like a nice, racist pint.

Mike   Guinness? What's racist about that?

Leo   The white's always on top.

    Leo MOVES AWAY TO A TABLE. *Mike* TAKES THE CHANGE FROM THE *Barman* AND FOLLOWS.

    CUT TO: ANOTHER ANGLE. *Mike* JOINS *Leo* AT A TABLE.

Leo   Hey – there is something you can do for me, Mike.

Mike   Sure.

Leo   I need a spark plug for the bike.

    Leo HOLDS TWO FINGERS APART.

Leo   You know an LB70?

Mike   No problem.

Leo   You won't get into any trouble?

Mike   For a spark plug? There's no problem, OK?

Leo   Thanks.

Mike   Cheers!

Leo   Yeah.

THEY CLINK GLASS AND DRINK.

CUT TO:

SCENE TWENTY-EIGHT

Fourth insert

A STREET. NIGHT. THE BRICK SPINS THROUGH THE NIGHT SKY, SOUNDLESSLY MAKING ITS WAY FROM *Mike's* HAND.

CUT TO:

SCENE TWENTY-NINE

Int. McClintock's office 3.00 p.m.

Mike STANDS IN FRONT OF *McClintock*. THE *Foreman* IS BY THE DOOR. THE SPARK PLUG IS ON THE DESK.

McClintock   Thank you, Clive.

THE *Foreman* LEAVES.

McClintock   So, what have you got to say for yourself?

Mike   It was just a spark plug.

McClintock   It's still pilfering.

Mike   But it's only worth . . .

McClintock   I know what it's worth, laddie.

Mike   It was for my mate, Leo. For his bike.

McClintock   Aye. Well, I think I warned you about making the wrong sort of associations, didn't I?

Mike   Yeah. Well, he's not a Rotarian, is he?

McClintock   And what's that meant to mean?

A PAUSE. *Mike* DOESN'T ANSWER.

McClintock   All right, Williams. You're out!

Mike   What?

McClintock	You heard me.
Mike	You're firing me!
McClintock	No. You don't have a job here. I'm *releasing* you.
Mike	What for?
McClintock	For stealing.
Mike	What about you? You and Sloane? Fiddling on the VAT …
McClintock	You watch your tongue, you little guttersnipe.
Mike	What's the difference?
McClintock	The difference is I'm a self-made business man. And you're a petty thief. The difference is that society needs people like me. But you're still wet behind the ears. I bend the rules. You break them. And your in no position to do that, son.
Mike	You mean I've got to wait until I'm a hypocritical, bigoted racist.
McClintock	Get out of here!
Mike	Yeah. You can get your slave labour from someone else.

Mike STORMS OUT OF THE OFFICE. *McClintock* MOVES
SLOWLY TO THE DOOR.

CUT TO: ANOTHER ANGLE. THE *Foreman* IS STANDING ON
THE OTHER SIDE. HE HAS HEARD EVERYTHING.

McClintock	Kids! Take them in. Give them a good training. And what do you get back?

CUT TO:

SCENE   THIRTY ░░░░░░░░░░░░░░░░░░░░░░░░░░

Ext. Street near garage 10.00 p.m.

Mike AND *Leo* ARE SITTING IN THE RUBBLE OF A BUILDING
SITE. THEY ARE SMOKING A JOINT, PASSING IT BACK AND
FORTH. THEY ARE BOTH STONED.

Mike	Of course – he's right.

4t 4t 4t 4t 4t 4t

Leo Right.

Mike The self-made man. And he can make himself anything he wants to be.

Leo Forget him, man. I'm just sorry I got you into trouble.

Mike I'm glad. I'm really glad.

Leo You are?

Mike I don't want anything of what he's got. I want out of it.

Leo You are out of it.

Mike Yeah. And staying out. If that's what 'society' wants, that seems like a good excuse for being anti-social. You get me?

Leo Nope.

Mike AND *Leo* LAUGH. THE JOKE ISN'T FUNNY, BUT THE DOPE HAS MADE IT SEEM SO.

Mike I'll show you.

CUT TO: ANOTHER ANGLE. *Mike* GETS UP AND LOOKS AROUND THE BUILDING SITE. THIS TIES IN WITH THE FIRST INSERT.

Mike Come on!

CUT TO:

SCENE   THIRTY-ONE

Ext. Outside McClintock's office 10.00 p.m.

PERHAPS THE OFFICE IS CLOSE TO THE BUILDING SITE, IT DOESN'T MATTER. *Mike* AND *Leo* ARE SUDDENLY THERE, OUT OF CONTROL, TOTALLY STONED.

Mike I'll show you.

THE THREE OTHER INSERTS. IN SLOW MOTION, *Mike* THROWS THE BRICK.

CUT TO: ANOTHER ANGLE. NOW WE SEE THE TARGET – A BEAUTIFUL WINDOW, ALMOST VICTORIAN IN STYLE. ON IT, WE CAN READ: 'IAN McCLINTOCK AND COMPANY LTD.

AUTOREPAIRS. ESTABLISHED 1955'.

CUT TO: ANOTHER ANGLE. THE BRICK TAKES AN AGE TO REACH THE WINDOW, TWISTING IN THE NIGHT AIR.

CUT TO: ANOTHER ANGLE. THE BRICK SMASHES THROUGH THE WINDOW. A TERRIBLE CLATTER AS THE GLASS FALLS IN SLOW MOTION. AN ALARM BELL RINGS.

CUT TO: CLOSE SHOT ON *Mike*. HE IS HAPPY. THIS IS, AT LAST, SOME SORT OF POSITIVE STATEMENT.

Leo   Come on, man!

Leo HAS BEEN SHAKEN BY THE REALISATION OF WHAT *Mike* HAS JUST DONE.

CUT TO: ANOTHER ANGLE. *Mike* AND *Leo* RUN OFF DOWN THE DESERTED STREET.

CUT TO: END CREDITS.

Killers

CHARACTERS

John Williams
Sally Williams
Karen Williams
Mike Williams
Steve Williams
Leo Young
Maggie Lambert
Sharon Harwood
Mr Sloane
Magistrate
Newscaster
Manager
Customer

SCENE ONE ▨▨▨▨▨▨▨▨▨▨▨▨▨▨▨▨▨▨▨▨▨▨▨▨▨
Int. Courtroom 10.30 a.m.

THE PLAY OPENS IN THE REPRESENTATIONAL COURTROOM THAT WE HAVE SEEN TWICE BEFORE. AS BEFORE, THE WITNESS IN THE DOCK APPEARS LOST AND ISOLATED IN THE SURREAL DARKNESS AND SIZE OF THE PLACE. IN THIS INSTANCE, IT IS *John Williams* WHO IS BEING CROSS-EXAMINED. *Mike Williams* IS ALSO PRESENT, LISTENING.

Magistrate   Mr Williams. Would it be true to say that your son's troubles began around the time you lost your job?

John   Yes. But it wasn't just me who lost my job. The factory where I worked was closed down.

CUT TO:

SCENE TWO ▨▨▨▨▨▨▨▨▨▨▨▨▨▨▨▨▨▨▨▨▨▨▨▨▨
Ext. QT-Pie Dolls Ltd 11.00 a.m.

OUTSIDE THE FACTORY GATES, A CROWD OF STRIKERS BLOCK A LORRY THAT IS TRYING TO ENTER. THERE ARE CLASHES WITH POLICE. RIOT SHIELDS AND TRUNCHEONS ARE IN USE.

Newscaster   [v/o] . . . outside the QT-Pie doll factory after Management attempts to move vital stock were disrupted by pickets. This is the third time that violence has flared since the factory was shut down two months ago.

CUT TO: CLOSE SHOT ON *John*, HE IS PICKED OUT AMONGST A GROUP OF STRIKERS INTERVIEWED BY AN UNSEEN REPORTER.

Reporter   [v/o] Does it worry you that you're now acting outside the law?

John   The law? Whose law? This company got a grant to move north, a grant to put three hundred people out of work. Now they've got a court order to keep us out. But what about *our* rights?

CUT TO:

SCENE THREE ░░░░░░░░░░░░░░░░░░░

Int. Courtroom 10.35 a.m.

THE CROSS-EXAMINATION CONTINUES.

John   I'd been working there for nearly twenty years . . .

Magistrate   But this was the first time you found yourself in direct conflict with the law?

John   I don't see . . .

Magistrate   Just answer the question, please, Mr Williams.

John   I don't understand the question.

CUT TO: CLOSE SHOT ON *Mike*. HE IS LISTENING INTENTLY. DOES HE BLAME HIS FATHER FOR WHAT HAPPENED?

Magistrate   [v/o] Your son is charged with a serious offence, Mr Williams. A criminal offence.

CUT TO: RESUME ON *Magistrate*.

Magistrate   I am simply trying to take every circumstance into consideration. And I think your own circumstances at the time . . .

John   So it's my fault, is it? Is that what you're trying to say?

Magistrate   You were closest to him.

John   I talked to him. I did everything I could. But we were never close.

Magistrate   But you must have set some sort of example to him.

John   Yes. I did.

CUT TO:

SCENE FOUR ░░░░░░░░░░░░░░░░░░░

Int. Williams' home (kitchen) 8.30 p.m.

John PRODUCES A BRAND NEW PERSONAL STEREO SYSTEM AND THROWS IT DOWN ON THE TABLE.

John   Where did you get it?

Mike	You've been in my room.
John	'Your' room? Who pays the mortgage for this place? Who pays the rates? I go where I please, laddy.
Mike	It's still my room. I've got a right to privacy.
John	Rights? Don't talk to me about rights. You gave up your rights the day you walked out of your job. Now, answer the question. Where did you get it?
Mike	What's it to you?
John	You stole it.
Mike	No!
John	Don't lie to me. What did it cost? Thirty quid? Forty? You don't have that sort of money.
Mike	I've got my savings.
John	You've drunk and smoked your savings. You haven't got anything.

CUT TO: ANOTHER ANGLE. *John* FORCES HIMSELF TO SPEAK CALMLY. HE DOESN'T WANT A ROW. HE WANTS TO HELP.

| John | Look, Mike – you want to waste your life, that's your choice. I haven't put any pressure on you. But if you're going to come up against the law ... |
| Mike | Me? You're a fine one to be talking. |

AND NOW *John* IS ANGRY AGAIN.

John	What do you mean by that?
Mike	You know what I mean. The factory ...
John	That's ...
Mike	They took out an injunction, didn't they! You're not allowed to be there any more. But you're still there.
John	What I'm doing, I'm doing for *you*. It's not just about my job. It's about jobs for you – for the next generation.
Mike	Come off it, dad!

Mike SNATCHES UP THE STEREO.

| Mike | You don't give a damn about me. You don't even know |

me. You think I'm a thief. You think I've been shop-
lifting.

John And you haven't?

Mike No. Sharon lent it to me.

Mike FLICKS IT OPEN. *Sharon's* NAME IS WRITTEN ON TAPE
INSIDE THE LID.

CUT TO:

SCENE FIVE ▨▨▨▨▨▨▨▨▨▨▨▨▨▨▨▨▨▨

Int. Courtroom 10.40 a.m.

Magistrate You argued?

John [TIREDLY] Yes.

Magistrate And I am correct on this point, Mr Williams. Your son
had never been in any trouble before. Not until you ...

CUT TO: CLOSE SHOT ON *John*

John [INTERRUPTING] Wait a minute. Hold on. Let's get one
thing straight. Just who's on trial?

John STABS A FINGER AT HIS SON.

John Him or me?

CUT TO:

SCENE SIX ▨▨▨▨▨▨▨▨▨▨▨▨▨▨▨▨▨▨▨

Opening credits

DISSOLVE TO:

SCENE SEVEN ▦▦▦▦▦▦▦▦▦▦▦▦▦▦▦▦▦▦▦▦▦▦▦▦▦▦

Ext. QT-Pie Dolls Ltd 11.00 a.m.

THE FACTORY IS EMPTY NOW. A BULLDOZER WAITS TO
DEMOLISH IT. *John* AND *Sally* WALK PAST THE LOCKED
GATES.

Sally   So it's all over?

John   Yeah – five weeks of picketing and what have we got to
show for it?

Sally   You've got more redundancy money.

John   A buy out. Fifteen per cent – that's all it took and we just
walked away. Sure, we got more money. But what's left?
They go to their nice redevelopment in Scotland, and
another piece of local industry is killed off for good.

Sally   Why do you blame yourself?

John   Because we helped them kill it. I suppose I shouldn't
have expected anything else. Our jobs. Our future. Our
lives. They're up for sale like everything else.

Sally   Come on, John . . .

John   Gas. Water. Electricity. Air. You find me one thing in
this country that isn't for sale.

Sally AND *John* WALK AWAY. BEHIND THEM, THE
BULLDOZER ROARS TO LIFE.

CUT TO:

SCENE EIGHT ▦▦▦▦▦▦▦▦▦▦▦▦▦▦▦▦▦▦▦▦▦▦▦▦

Int. An amusement arcade 12.30 p.m.

CLOSE SHOT: THIS IS ONE OF THOSE KUNG-FU GAMES,
WHERE AN ANIMATED FIGURE KICKS AND CHOPS ITS WAY
THROUGH A SERIES OF ASSASSINS. WE DON'T SEE (YET)
WHAT THE GAME IS CALLED. THE HERO-FIGURE IS DOING
WELL. THE SCORE IS RISING. THEN ONE OF THE ASSASSINS
GETS IT AND THE GAME IS OVER.

CUT TO: WIDER ANGLE.

Mike HAS BEEN PLAYING THE GAME. *Leo* HAS BEEN WATCHING. NOW HE BASHES THE MACHINE AND SPINS ROUND.

Mike   Hell! I only needed another hundred points and I'd have got a free game.

Leo   You going to play that thing all day?

Mike   You got any better idea?

Leo   I need food, man.

Mike   You got any money?

Leo   Sure. I got plenty money.

Leo GESTURES AT THE MACHINE.

Leo   The trouble is, you've put it all in there.

Mike   You want a go?

Leo   Wipe out an army and win a pizza?

Mike   It's my treat! Come on ...

THE TWO OF THEM MAKE THEIR WAY OUT OF THE AMUSEMENT ARCADE.

CUT TO:

SCENE NINE

Int. Fast food restaurant 2.00 p.m.

Mike AND *Leo* ARE EATING PIZZAS IN A FAST FOOD RESTAURANT. THEY ARE CLOSE TO THE DOOR. THEIR MEAL IS ALMOST OVER.

Mike   What would you do for money?

Leo   What wouldn't I do?

Mike   No. I'm talking about easy money.

Leo   No such thing.

Mike   Listen. I was down the pub last week, right? The Four Feathers. And this old bird came in. Had a half of Guinness and then left. Are you with me?

Leo   What? She bought you a Guinness, too?

Mike   No. It's just, some of the punters were talking about her . . .

CUT TO:

SCENE TEN ▦▦▦▦▦▦▦▦▦▦▦▦▦▦▦▦▦▦▦▦

Ext. Maggie Lambert's house   4.00 p.m.

Maggie Lambert WALKS HOME, CARRYING HER SHOPPING. SHE GOES INTO THE FRONT DOOR.

Mike   [v/o] Apparently, she's really stacked. She's got hundreds of pounds.

Leo   [v/o] In the bank?

Mike   [v/o] No. That's just the thing.

CUT TO:

SCENE ELEVEN ▦▦▦▦▦▦▦▦▦▦▦▦▦▦▦▦▦▦

Int. Maggie's bedroom   2.15 p.m.

Maggie GOES INTO A SMALL, COMFORTABLE AND WELL-DECORATED BEDROOM. SHE APPROACHES THE BED.

Mike   [v/o] You know what old people are like. Keeps it under the mattress, doesn't she?

Maggie TURNS THE MATTRESS UP. THERE ARE HUNDREDS OF POUNDS UNDERNEATH IT, ALL CRISP NEW FIVERS. SHE TAKES OUT A WAD AND BEGINS TO COUNT IT.

Mike   [v/o] Likes to count it last thing before she goes to bed.

CUT TO:

SCENE TWELVE ▦▦▦▦▦▦▦▦▦▦▦▦▦▦▦▦▦▦

Int. Fast food restaurant   2.20 p.m.

AS BEFORE.

Leo   You're kidding me.

Mike   That's what they said.

Leo   No. I mean – you wouldn't . . .

Mike   Why not?

Leo   An old lady!

Mike   She doesn't need it.

Leo   Do you?

Mike   I'm skint.

Leo   Then how are you going to pay for this?

Mike   You finished?

Leo   Yeah.

Mike LOOKS ROUND THE RESTAURANT. THERE ARE NO WAITERS OR WAITRESSES NEAR THEM.

Mike   Now!

Mike GETS UP AND MOVES QUICKLY OUT OF THE FRONT DOOR – WITHOUT PAYING.

Leo   Mike!

Leo HAS NO CHOICE THIS TIME. HE GETS UP AND FOLLOWS.

CUT TO: ANOTHER ANGLE. THE *Manager* SEES THEM GO.

Manager   Oy!

THE *Manager* SPRINTS FOR THE DOOR.

CUT TO:

SCENE THIRTEEN

Ext. A street 3.00 p.m.

Mike AND *Leo* HAVEN'T BEEN CAUGHT. THEY COME TO A BREATHLESS HALT BESIDE A BENCH.

Leo   You crazy, man?

Mike   What's the matter?

Leo	You could have told me . . .
Mike	Told you what?
Leo	That you were going to do a runner.
Mike	We weren't caught.
Leo	We weren't?

A PAUSE *Leo* CONSIDERS.

Leo	I'm through with this, Mike.
Mike	Through?
Leo	Yeah. I'm gonna get a job.
Mike	What sort of job?
Leo	Waiting.
Mike	Waiting for what?
Leo	Waiting in a restaurant.
Mike	You don't want to be a waiter.
Leo	I got to do something, Mike. You and me . . . we're just killing time. Only, sometimes I think that it's time that's killing us.
Mike	That's deep!
Leo	Yeah – like the pizzas.
Mike	But why, Leo?
Leo	I just want to be in control of my own life for a while.
Mike	And putting on a funny hat and wiping tables is the way to do it?

A BRIEF PAUSE AS THEY WAIT FOR TWO PEOPLE TO WALK PAST.

Leo	You think you're in control right now?
Mike	You tell me.
Leo	I've been in trouble before, Mike. I know where we're going – and it's a one-way street. If it's a choice of a funny hat or blue denim with a number on my chest, I know which one I want.
Mike	We're not going to get nicked!

Leo   That's what they all say. Then they get nicked. Anyway, it's different for you. You're only sixteen. I'm eighteen.

Mike   You're a man, man! [PAUSE]   So when do you start?

Leo   Next week.

Mike   You know, you're right. It's just a big game, isn't it? Life. A game for six billion players. Throw a dice to start. Yeah – it's all luck, isn't it? Throw a one and you start off in the Third World – Ethiopia. John Paul Getty must have thrown a twelve. I suppose you and me . . . what do you think? We got a two or a three.

Leo   Mike . . .

Mike   The winner is the first one to pass a hundred. Go straight to your funeral. Do no pass 'Go'. Do not collect your state pension . . .

Leo   I didn't make the rules.

Mike   No. So that's why we *break* the rules. Sod the game! We do things our own way.

Leo   No. You do it your way, Mike. I'm doing it mine . . .

Leo WALKS AWAY. *Mike* STARES AFTER HIM.

Mike   Leo . . .

Leo DOESN'T TURN ROUND. *Mike* CALLS AGAIN.

Mike   Leo!

CUT TO:

SCENE   FOURTEEN   ▨▨▨▨▨▨▨▨▨▨▨▨▨▨▨▨▨▨▨▨▨▨▨

Ext. An office in the city 4.30 p.m.

John STEPS OUT OF A SMALL OFFICE IN A BUSY STREET. HE IS CARRYING A BRIEFCASE AND THERE'S A SPRING IN HIS STEP. ABOUT TWO WEEKS HAVE PASSED SINCE THE SCENE OUTSIDE THE FACTORY.

CUT TO:

SCENE FIFTEEN

Int. Williams' home (living room) 4.45 p.m.

Sally IS IRONING. SHE IS SURPRISED TO SEE *John* COME IN.

John Hello, love.

Sally You're home early. How did it go?

John Here ...

John GIVES HER A TEN-POUND NOTE.

John I want to have the whole family round for lunch this weekend. We'll have a joint of something. All right?

Sally They liked your idea!

John We're in business!

Sally Oh, John!

Sally EMBRACES HIM.

Sally So when do you start?

John Give me time. It's only been two weeks since they closed down the factory. It's going to take me time to get used to the idea.

Sally Being your own boss.

John It's more than that.

John PERCHES ON THE ARM OF A SOFA.

John We did everything we could to keep the factory open – but nobody listened to us. They just didn't care. But you know what I say? To hell with them! From now on, I'm going to be looking out for myself.

Sally You don't need anyone else.

John That's just it. You can't beat the system. The government. Politicians. Stuff the lot of 'em. You've just got to look after number one.

Sally UNFOLDS THE TEN-POUND NOTE.

Sally I'll get a chicken.

John And some sparkly – eh? I've got my own business now. And I promise you this – We're going to make a killing.

CUT TO:

SCENE SIXTEEN ▩▩▩▩▩▩▩▩▩▩▩▩▩▩▩▩▩▩▩

Ext. Outside Karen's flat 8.00 a.m.

Steve IS HELPING *Karen* PAINT SOME PLACARDS FOR A DEMONSTRATION. THESE READ: 'STOP ACID RAIN' AND (MORE ENIGMATIC) 'THIRTY PER CENT!'.

Karen You know – it's crazy. I keep on having nightmares about it.

Steve About the protest?

Karen No, about the ecology. I'm in the North Pole. You're there. So are mum and dad and Mike. I've seen this great big hole in the sky and I want to telephone somebody about it. Only nobody cares. Nobody wants to know.

Steve A hole?

Karen It's not as stupid as it sounds. It's there. It was discovered by a scientist called Farman back in 1985. A hole in the ozone layer.

Steve So what happens . . . in the dream?

Karen I find a telephone – but it's been vandalised. Then I wake up.

Steve FINISHES HIS POSTER. THIS IS THE ONE THAT READS, 'THIRTY PER CENT!'.

Steve There. It's finished.

Karen It's good.

Steve Yeah. What does it mean?

Karen Thirty per cent. Did you know that England is the dirtiest country in Europe?

Steve LOOKS AROUND.

Steve Is it?

Karen Our power stations are putting more sulphur into the atmosphere than all the volcanoes in the world put together.

Steve	That's bad?
Karen	You ever heard of acid rain? It's a killer. Lakes, rivers, forests. Fish. Animals. It's killing everything.
Steve	What about the thirty per cent?
Karen	That's what we're protesting about. We want the government to cut down sulphur emissions by thirty per cent, like the rest of Europe. But they won't do it.
Steve	Why not?
Karen	Because it would cost money. And they're too busy making money to care.
	CUT TO:

SCENE SEVENTEEN

Ext. A street/Karen's car 12.00 p.m.

Steve AND *Karen* AT THE END OF THE DEMO ARE GETTING INTO THE CAR. TWO OR THREE EXTRAS WITH PLACARDS WALK PAST AND SAY GOODBYE. THE DEMONSTRATION GEAR IS IN THE BACK.

Karen	I can see I haven't exactly impressed you.
Steve	It's none of my business.
Karen	It's your world.
Steve	Says who?
Karen	You really amaze me sometimes, Steve. If kids don't care about ecology, then who will? Don't you want to grow up in a world with trees and fields ...
Steve	It's not as bad as that.
Karen	Get the facts, Steve. It's worse. Look ...

CUT TO: ANOTHER ANGLE. THE CAR PASSES ONE OF THOSE CRAZY SANDWICH-BOARD MEN. HE'S HOLDING UP A SIGN: 'THE END OF THE WORLD IS NIGH'.

RESUME ON *Karen* AND *Steve*.

Steve	A nutter ...

Karen Yeah. The trouble is, he may have a point.

CUT TO:

SCENE EIGHTEEN

Ext./Int. Outside Williams' home 12.30 p.m.

Mike WALKS INTO THE DRIVE AS *Karen* AND *Steve* GET OUT OF THE CAR.

Karen Hello, Mike. You joining us, then?

Mike Yeah – it's the big celebration. Hi, Steve.

Karen I'll see you inside.

Karen GOES INTO THE HOUSE.

CUT TO: ANOTHER ANGLE. *Steve* AND *Mike* ARE LEFT ALONE.

Steve I didn't think you'd come.

Mike A free meal? Of course, if you don't want me ...

Steve You're not going to have another row with dad, are you?

Mike Don't worry. I'm on my best behaviour. No glue sniffing at the table. If you want to leave the table to OD on heroin, ask permission first.

Steve You're not into all that, are you?

Mike You don't think so, do you?

Steve Are you?

Mike 'Course not. I may be stupid, but I'm not as thick as all that.

A PAUSE. *Mike* CONSIDERS HIS YOUNGER BROTHER.

Mike So how's school, then?

Steve It's all right.

A PAUSE.

Steve How about you?

Mike What about me?

68

Steve   You know.

ANOTHER PAUSE.

Steve   Dad's getting really worried.

Mike   Yeah. Dad's always worried. I don't know what makes him think it's any of his business.

CUT TO: ANOTHER ANGLE. *Karen* CALLS FROM THE FRONT DOOR.

Karen   Steve! Mike!

CUT TO: RESUME ON *Steve* AND *Mike*.

Mike   Actually, I'm about to come into a bit of money.

Steve   You got a job.

Mike   Not exactly. It's sort of more like a private commission.

Steve   What do you mean?

Mike   Well, I may be doing some travelling soon. Abroad.

Steve   Where?

Mike   I haven't made up my mind. But I'm not wasting my time in this shit-hole. Are you coming in?

Steve   Yeah.

Mike   Don't mention it to them – OK?

Steve   Why not?

Mike   I don't know. It may come to nothing ...

Mike AND *Steve* WALK INTO THE HOUSE TOGETHER.

CUT TO:

SCENE NINETEEN

Int. Williams' home (kitchen) 1.00 p.m.

Sally SQUIRTS AIR FRESHENER (FROM AN AEROSOL CAN) AROUND THE KITCHEN. THE JOINT IS READY TO BE CARVED.

CUT TO:

SCENE TWENTY ██████████████████████████████

Int. Williams' home (dining room) 1.15 p.m.

Sally CARRIES THE JOINT INTO THE DINING ROOM. *John*, *Mike*, *Steve* AND *Karen* ARE ALREADY SITTING ROUND THE TABLE. *John* PROUDLY DISPLAYS A HAMBURGER CARTON, SHAPED LIKE AN ANIMAL.

John	There it is! The zoo-pack.
Steve	It's horrible!
Karen	What is it?
John	It's a hamburger container. Kids will love it.
Steve	I don't love it!
Sally	You're not a kid!
Karen	Go on, dad.
John	Right. You know I got paid off when the factory went – OK? So I decided there's no point sitting around here. Not without any work. So me and a couple of mates have gone into business for ourselves.
Karen	You've put your money into *that*?
John	Some of it. But the point is, we can get a government grant. You know – one of those enterprise schemes. So we manufacture these, and flog them to a big hamburger chain. And that's just the start . . .
Karen	Zoo-packs.
John	Lions are just the first off the line. We've got a prototype zebra, a giraffe, a monkey and a corgi.
Steve	A corgi?
John	For hot-dogs.

CUT TO: ANOTHER ANGLE. *Karen* REACHES OUT AND PICKS UP THE CARTON. *Sally* IS SERVING THE FOOD.

Karen	It's styrofoam.
John	Well, what do you expect?
Karen	These things are lethal, dad. They're killers!

John   What are you talking about?

Karen   Every time you step on a styrofoam carton, you release about a million balloons of toxic waste.

John   And what do they do? Float around looking for a funfair?

Steve   Oh no!

Karen   No. That's what I've been having nightmares about. It's these things that are destroying the ozone layer – up there.

SHE POINTS.

Karen   Polystyrene, aerosols, industrial solvents . . . they're making a hole in our atmosphere.

Sally   I don't see what that's got to do with your father, dear.

Karen   Well, it might have something to do with him when we all start dying of cancer.

Mike   What a load of . . .

Sally   Michael!

John   What is all this? You're looking at me like I'm some sort of killer, myself!

Steve   She's got ecology on the brain!

Mike   Greenpeace? Yurrch . . .

Karen   Can't you see? I'm not knocking you, dad. Of course I want your business to do well. But that's what we're demonstrating about. A hole in the sky. Rivers with no fish. Forests with no trees.

Karen PICKS UP THE CARTON.

Karen   This is where it all starts!

Sally   If this is going to turn into another argument, I'm leaving!

Steve   Me too.

Mike   Yeah. And me.

CUT TO: ANGLE FAVOURING *John*. HE IS CLOSE TO ANGER, BUT HE CONTROLS HIMSELF.

John   This isn't an argument. This is a discussion. Right?   [TO *Karen*]   Right?

Karen	Right.
John	I'm no killer, Karen. I'm doing what any man in my position would do – I'm trying to do the best for my family.

You talk about the world – but look at my world. Look at Mike's world. We've got nothing. We have to look after ourselves. All right – you're going out demonstrating about the big bad bureaucrats who are polluting the rivers and the forests. That's fine. But don't tar me with the same brush. I'm just a little guy with my own business. I'm not one of them.

Karen	But what happens when the little guy becomes the big guy, dad?
John	That's when you come hammering on my door.
Karen	But that's when it's too late.
Sally	Karen, darling . . .
Karen	Yes, mother?
Sally	What's the worst pollution, would you say? Exhaust fumes or these hamburger cartons?
Karen	Why?
Sally	I'm just interested . . .
Karen	Well, they're as bad as each other.
Sally	Right – well, before you have another go at your father, why don't you tell us how you got here today?

Karen BITES HER LIP.

CUT TO:

SCENE TWENTY-ONE ░░░░░░░░░░░░░░░░░░░░░░░░░░░░

Ext. Williams' home 2.00 p.m.

Karen's CAR IS PARKED OUTSIDE THE HOUSE. THE BANNERS ARE VISIBLE THROUGH THE BACK WINDOW.

CUT TO: CLOSE SHOT ON *Karen's* EXHAUST PIPE.

CUT TO: AN EXTENDED MONTAGE WITH A MUSIC TRACK

THAT SHOULD BE WRITTEN SPECIALLY ON THE THEME OF
'KILLERS'. THE POINT? WE'RE ALL KILLERS. KILLING IS PART
OF LIFE. THE ACTION SHOULD BE FILMED LIKE A POP VIDEO.
IF POSSIBLE, THE FOLLOWING IMAGES (SOME OF THEM
FROM THIS EPISODE) COULD BE INTERCUT WITH THE MAIN
ACTION:

- THE CHICKEN (OR JOINT) BEING CHOPPED.
- *Sally* WITH HER AEROSOL CAN.
- THE SANDWICH-BOARD MAN.
- THE NIGHT SKY.
- A GORY SHOT FROM A WAR FILM.
- LAYING A WREATH AT THE CENOTAPH (STOCK FOOTAGE).
- THE KILLERS IN THE ENTERTAINMENT MACHINE.
- ACID RAIN DAMAGED TREES
- DEAD FISH.
- SMOKE STACKS BILLOWING OUT POLLUTION.

DISSOLVE TO:

SCENE TWENTY-TWO

Int. Fast food restaurant 3.00 p.m.

Leo IS WORKING ON THE PRODUCTION LINE, GRILLING
HAMBURGERS, DRESSED IN THE COSTUME OF A
MCDONALD'S OR A WIMPEY OUTLET. IT IS SLOW, BORING
WORK. WE CAN ALMOST SMELL THE FAT. HE PUTS A
DOLLOP OF KETCHUP ON A COMPLETED HAMBURGER.

Customer   One super burger without ketchup.

Leo PICKS UP THE PIECE OF MEAT AND WIPES OFF THE
KETCHUP WITH A CLOTH. HE REASSEMBLES THE FINISHED
PRODUCT.

Customer   And no gherkins.

HE OPENS IT UP, PULLS OUT THE GHERKINS AND CLOSES IT
AGAIN.

Customer   Wholemeal bun.

THE HAMBURGER IS IN THE WRONG BUN. *Leo* PULLS IT
APART AND PUTS IT IN THE RIGHT BUN. HE IS LOSING HIS
COOL. AT LAST HE'S GOT IT RIGHT, THOUGH. HE PUTS THE

FINISHED HAMBURGER IN A CARTON AND CARRIES IT
FORWARD.

CUT TO:

SCENE TWENTY-THREE ▦▦▦▦▦▦▦▦▦▦▦▦

Ext. Restaurant service exit 3.30 p.m.

Leo WALKS OUT. *Mike* IS WAITING FOR HIM.

Leo   That's not a living. That's a dying!

CUT TO:

SCENE TWENTY-FOUR ▦▦▦▦▦▦▦▦▦▦▦▦▦

Ext. Maggie's house 3.45 p.m.

A HOUSE AT THE END OF A TERRACE IN A SMALL STREET.
Maggie GOES OUT WITH HER SHOPPING BAG, LOCKING THE
DOOR.

CUT TO: ANOTHER ANGLE. *Mike* AND *Leo* ARE WATCHING.

Mike   Told you. She always goes out around now. Shopping.

Leo   How long?

Mike   About an hour. I've been watching her for a week, Leo.

Leo   And you're sure. About the money?

Mike   Under the mattress. In a tin in the kitchen. We'll find it.

Leo HESITATES.

Mike   We'll be ten minutes. Straight in. Straight out.

Leo DECIDES.

Leo   Right.

THE TWO OF THEM CROSS THE ROAD.

CUT TO:

SCENE   TWENTY-FIVE
Int. Amusement arcade 4.00 p.m.

A CAMERA SLOWLY PANS IN ON THE ENTERTAINMENT
MACHINE THAT *Mike* WAS PLAYING AT THE START OF THE
PLAY. NOW WE SEE ITS NAME, 'KILLERS', AND *Mike* AND *Leo*
ARE ON THE SCREEN. ON THE SOUNDTRACK, AN ECHO FROM
SCENE EIGHT.

Mike   [v/o] It's just a big game, isn't it? Life. A game for six
billion players.

THE COMPUTERISED FIGURES HAVE ENTERED THE HOUSE.
SUDDENLY, A RED SQUARE FLASHES ON THE SCREEN.

Mike   [v/o] Sod the game! We do things our own way.

DISSOLVE TO:

SCENE   TWENTY-SIX
Int. Maggie's home (sitting room) 4.10 p.m.

THE RED LIGHT BECOMES THE RED COVER OF *Maggie's* BUS
PASS. SHE HAS LEFT IT BEHIND.

CUT TO: ANOTHER ANGLE. A WINDOW AT THE BACK OF
THE ROOM IS FORCED OPEN. *Mike* CLIMBS IN. *Leo* IS RIGHT
BEHIND HIM.

CUT TO:

SCENE   TWENTY-SEVEN
Ext. A street 4.15 p.m.

Maggie REALISES THAT SHE HAS LEFT HER BUS PASS
BEHIND. SHE TURNS ROUND, AND GOES TO GET IT.

CUT TO:

SCENE TWENTY-EIGHT

Int. Maggie's house (sitting room) 4.20 p.m.

Mike AND *Leo* ARE SEARCHING THROUGH THE ROOM, BEING NONE TOO CAREFUL WITH *Maggie's* POSSESSIONS. THE ROOM IS VERY DIFFERENT TO ANYTHING WE SAW IN *Mike's* VISION (SCENE NINE). *Maggie* HAS NO SAVINGS. SHE LIVES IN POVERTY, SURROUNDED BY A FEW TATTERED MEMORIES. ON A TABLE, THERE'S A PHOTOGRAPH OF HER DEAD HUSBAND, A SOLDIER FROM THE SECOND WORLD WAR.

Leo   There's nothing here, man. It's just a waste of time.

Mike   Sh ...

Mike LASHES OUT ANGRILY. HE SMASHES THE PHOTOGRAPH.

Leo   Hey – there's no need for that.

Mike   Let's split.

CUT TO:

SCENE TWENTY-NINE

Ext. Maggie's house 4.30 p.m.

Maggie REACHES THE FRONT DOOR AND OPENS IT. SHE GOES IN. THE CAMERA FREEZES ON THE SCENE.

CUT TO:

SCENE THIRTY ░░░░░░░░░░░░░░░░░░░░░░░░░░░░░

A FAST MONTAGE OF IMAGES IN BLACK AND WHITE.
- A FLASH GOES OFF. THE BODY OF *Maggie* LIES ON THE FLOOR OF HER SITTING ROOM.
- ANOTHER FLASH. *Maggie* ON A STRETCHER.
- A PHOTOGRAPH OF *Maggie* IN A NEWSPAPER.
- A HEADLINE. 'KILLERS'.
- ANOTHER PHOTOGRAPH. A POLICE OUTLINE OF THE BODY OF *Maggie* WHERE IT WAS FOUND.
- THE BROKEN PHOTOGRAPH OF THE SOLDIER.

CUT TO:

SCENE THIRTY-ONE ░░░░░░░░░░░░░░░░░░░░░░░░░░

Ext. Maggie's house 4.45 p.m.

BACK TO THE PRESENT. *Leo* AND *Mike* SUDDENLY APPEAR, RUNNING OUT OF THE HOUSE. WE CAN'T BE SURE WHAT HAPPENED INSIDE THE HOUSE, BUT THEY ARE FAR FROM BEING 'KILLERS'. THEY ARE PANICKING, TERRIFIED BY WHATEVER HAS HAPPENED.

CUT TO: ANOTHER ANGLE. THEY RUN AWAY, DISAPPEARING DOWN THE STREET. BEHIND THEM, WE SEE A HUGE CIGARETTE ADVERTISEMENT. THE GOVERNMENT HEALTH WARNING ('SMOKING KILLS') LOOMS LARGE BEHIND THEM.

CUT TO: END CREDITS.

As Seen on TV

Captions

THIS SHOULD BE A 'SECOND GENERATION' SHOT – I.E. FILMED AS THEY'RE FLASHED ONTO A TV SCREEN. WE CAN PERHAPS MAKE OUT THE HORIZONTALS OF THE 'INNER' TV.

CAPTION 1: NINETY-EIGHT PER CENT IN THE U.K. HAVE A TV.
CAPTION 2: FIFTY PER CENT OF HOMES IN THE UK HAVE TWO TV'S OR MORE.
CAPTION 3: THE AVERAGE TEENAGER WATCHES 1248 HOURS OF TELEVISION EVERY YEAR.
CAPTION 4: WHY DO YOU BELIEVE THESE CAPTIONS?

DISSOLVE TO:

SCENE ONE
Int. Hospital room 11.00 a.m.

CLOSE SHOT: ON A TV SCREEN. IT IS BLANK FOR A MOMENT AND WE COULD THINK THAT IT'S AN ORDINARY TV SCREEN. BUT THEN, A SINGLE WHITE DOT PULSATES WEAKLY ACROSS WITH A BLEEP.

PULL BACK TO: WIDER ANGLE. THIS IS A PRIVATE ROOM IN A HOSPITAL – THE SAME HOSPITAL WHERE *Karen* WORKS. *Maggie* IS LYING THERE, DYING. THE TV SCREEN MONITORS HER HEARTBEAT.

CUT TO:

SCENE TWO
Ext. Outside Maggie's house 11.00 a.m.

THE HOUSE WHERE *Maggie* WAS ATTACKED HAS NOW BEEN CORDONED OFF BY THE POLICE. *Carrie Andrews*, A FREELANCE TV JOURNALIST, IS STANDING IN FRONT OF IT.

Carrie I'm standing outside 23 Broadwater Street where Maggie Lambert, an 87-year-old widow had lived for forty years.

CUT TO:

SCENE THREE ░░░░░░░░░░░░░░░░░░░░░░░░░░░░

Int. Cutting room 11.00 a.m.

> CLOSE SHOT: WE SEE THE SAME IMAGE OF *Carrie* FROM
> SEVERAL ANGLES – ON A BANK OF TV SCREENS. THERE IS
> CIGARETTE SMOKE IN THE ROOM, SUGGESTING THAT
> THERE'S SOMEONE THERE – BUT WE NEVER SEE A FACE. A
> *Producer,* WHO WILL REMAIN UNSEEN, IS HEARD.

Producer [v/o] Move in for a close shot.

> CUT TO:

SCENE FOUR ░░░░░░░░░░░░░░░░░░░░░░░░░░░░

Ext. Outside Maggie's house 11.00 a.m.

> *Carrie* CONTINUES AS BEFORE.

Carrie Yesterday, Maggie was brutally attacked in her own home
by two unidentified youths – yet another victim of inner-
city violence and lawlessness.

Producer [v/o] OK – three.

> CUT TO:

SCENE FIVE ░░░░░░░░░░░░░░░░░░░░░░░░░░░░

Int. Cutting room 11.00 a.m.

> WE'RE BACK INSIDE THE CUTTING ROOM. LOOKING AT
> IMAGES OF *Carrie*, THE HOSPITAL WHERE *Maggie* HAS BEEN
> TAKEN AND A STILL SHOT OF *Maggie* HERSELF. THE
> CASUAL, ALMOST BORED ATMOSPHERE IN THE FISH TANK
> CONTRASTS WITH THE URGENCY OF *Carrie's* MESSAGE.

Carrie The two men got away with just four pounds ...

Producer [v/o] Now, slowly pull back ...

> THE IMAGE ON THE OUTPUT SCREEN PULLS BACK FROM
> *Carrie*.

Carrie ... and now, frail, frightened Maggie Lambert is fighting for her life – in a critical condition, according to doctors.

Producer   [v/o] Frail and frightened, I like that. OK – one.

THE IMAGE ON THE OUTPUT SCREEN CUTS TO A BLACK AND WHITE PHOTOGRAPH OF *Maggie*.

Carrie   This is Maggie Lambert. A mother and a grand-mother ...

Producer   [v/o] Cue one.

THE OUTPUT SCREEN SWITCHES TO THE PHOTOGRAPH OF *Maggie*.

Carrie   Just another victim? Just another statistic?

Producer   [v/o] Great.

Carrie   No. Old Maggie Lambert's violent end must surely affect us all.

Producer   [v/o] And cut.

CUT TO:

SCENE   SIX

Ext. Outside Maggie's house 11.00 a.m.

AS BEFORE. BUT SUDDENLY, *Carrie's* CARING AND COMPASSIONATE MANNER EVAPORATES. SHE TALKS INTO CAMERA.

Carrie   Was that OK, Geoff, because I'm bloody freezing and I need a drink. OK?

CUT TO:

SCENE   SEVEN

Opening credits

FADE TO:

SCENE EIGHT ▦▦▦▦▦▦▦▦▦▦▦▦▦▦▦▦▦▦▦▦▦▦▦▦

Ext. A pub 7.00 p.m.

Leo AND *Mike* ARE SITTING IN A PUB – IN A QUIET CORNER. ON THE OTHER SIDE OF THE ROOM THERE'S A TV SCREEN – AND THE BROADCAST WE HAVE JUST SEEN BEING FILMED IS COMING TO A CLOSE.

Carrie   Just another victim? Just another statistic? No. Old Maggie Lambert's violent end must surely affect us all.

CUT TO: CLOSE SHOT ON *Mike* AND *Leo*. THEY ARE FORCED TO SPEAK IN LOW VOICES THROUGHOUT THIS DIALOGUE.

Mike   What are we going to do?

Leo   Nothing.

Mike   Nothing?

Leo   Nothing. There's nothing we can do. So we do nothing.

Mike   She may die. She may be dead already.

Leo   She's not dead.

Mike   You heard what she said. 'Fighting for her life.' That's what she said.

Leo   Yeah. That's what she said. To frighten us.

Mike   You don't believe her?

Leo   [LOUDLY] How do I know?

Leo REMEMBERS WHERE HE IS AND KEEPS HIS VOICE DOWN.

Mike   So what do we do?

Leo   I said . . .

Mike   Maybe we ought to go the police. Turn ourselves in.

Leo   Are you crazy?

Mike   It might be better for us.

Leo   Better? For you, maybe. What do you think the police are going to do if they get their hands on me?

Mike   It's the same for both of us.

Leo WHISPERS AS LOUDLY AS HE CAN.

Leo   That's just where you're wrong! I'm eighteen. You're sixteen. I'm a man. You're a kid. That's the law.

Mike   So what?

Leo   You go to juvenile court – nice and cushy. They won't even put your name in the papers. But that's not the point . . .

Leo DRINKS – AND FOR ONCE, THERE'S ALCOHOL IN HIS GLASS.

Leo   You're white. *That's* the point.

Mike   Wait a minute . . .

Leo   No. You wait a minute . . .

AGAIN, HIS VOICE WAS TOO LOUD. ONE OR TWO DRINKERS TURN ROUND AND NOTICE HIM. *Leo* PULLS HIMSELF TOGETHER AND SPEAKS MORE QUIETLY.

Leo   I've seen it. Black kids picked up in the street. No reason. Just picked up and put in the bull van and given a kicking. You ever hear of Trevor Monerville?

Mike   No.

Leo   He walked into a police station. But he came out on his back. They buried him with a fractured skull. And Colin Roach . . . He shot himself. That's what they said. Black people don't seem to last very long in white police stations, you know. They seem to have 'accidents'. They get their hands on me, I'm dead.

Mike   You don't believe that!

Leo   I've seen it!

Mike   Yeah?

Leo   OK. I know people who've seen it.

Mike   Yeah – well, that's different, innit?

Leo   What's different?

Mike   Look, Leo, we're in trouble. But all that stuff about the police. That's just crazy. Propaganda.

Leo   Says who?

Mike Look around you! This isn't Argentina, or Chile! They're just . . .

Leo Look. If you like the police so much, why don't you turn yourself in.

Mike I don't like the police. Nobody *likes* the police. I'm just saying we got enough to worry about without making them into monsters. Right?

A PAUSE. *Mike* CANNOT ARGUE WITH *Leo*. IT IS ALL OUTSIDE HIS OWN EXPERIENCE.

Mike You won't . . . do anything?

Leo We're in this together, man. Together!

Mike NODS. *Leo* LEAVES.

CUT TO:

SCENE NINE ▨▨▨▨▨▨▨▨▨▨▨▨▨▨▨▨▨▨▨▨▨▨

Ext. School playground 11.00 a.m.

Sonia IS WALKING WITH ONE OF THE KIDS – *Derek* – WHO ATTACKED *Steve* IN THE FIRST PLAY.

Sonia Now I know what a criminal must feel like.

Derek Like, what?

Sonia Like, guilty.

Derek What are you talking about?

Sonia Steve Williams. The way we're always on at him. Just because he's quiet. And because he likes ice-skating.

Derek Come off it, Sonia. He's a bloody poof, isn't he? Poncing around on the ice like Rupert bloody Nureyev.

Sonia It's Rudolf, actually.

Derek Oh, is it? Presenting Stevie Williams and Rudolf Nureyev in the dance of the Sugar Plum Fairy.

Derek DANCES AROUND *Sonia* IN AN EFFEMINATE MANNER, SINGING AT THE SAME TIME.

Sonia Oh, get off it, Derek.

Derek	What's got into you?

Derek What's got into you?

Sonia You've always got to have someone to pick on, haven't you?

Derek I don't know what you're going on about. It was only a joke.

Sonia Yeah, it's always a joke with you, isn't it? First the black kids, 'cos they're black. Then the Chinks, 'cos they're yellow. Then that spastic kid. Make you feel more of a man, does it?

Derek Leave it out, Sonia.

Sonia No, Derek. What's wrong with Steve, anyway? He likes ice-skating! There's nothing wrong with that.

Derek You're in a right mood, aren't you!

Sonia I just feel dirty, that's all . . .

THE TWO WALK ON TOGETHER.

CUT TO:

SCENE TEN

Int. Ice rink 7.00 p.m.

Steve IS SKATING. THERE ARE OTHER PEOPLE ON THE ICE BUT HE IS EASILY THE BEST SKATER IN THE ARENA. WE FOLLOW HIM AS HE DOES A SERIES OF LOOPS. THEN . . .

CUT TO: ANOTHER ANGLE. *Sonia* IS ALSO ON THE ICE. SHE CAN BARELY STAND UPRIGHT AND WOBBLES UNEASILY. *Steve* SEES HER. HE HESITATES. THEN (SEEING SHE IS PETRIFIED) HE SKATES EFFORTLESSLY OVER TO HER.

Steve What are you doing here?

Sonia What does it look like?

Steve You tell me.

Sonia I was watching you. You make it look so easy, I thought I'd try it for myself.

Steve IS SUSPICIOUS. HE REMEMBERS THE LAST TIME *Sonia* PRETENDED TO BE FRIENDLY.

Steve	So where's Derek, then?
Sonia	Derek?
Steve	Well, he put you up to this, didn't he?
	HE LOOKS AROUND HIM.
Steve	Where's he going to jump out from? Him and the others? Why don't you all just leave me alone?
	HE TURNS, AND IS ABOUT TO SKATE AWAY, BUT *Sonia* REACHES OUT WITH AN UNSTEADY HAND AND STOPS HIM.
Sonia	Steve – wait a minute.
Steve	What?
Sonia	I came to say, I'm sorry.
Steve	[UNBELIEVING] Yeah?
Sonia	Yeah. Really. Why else do you think I've come out on here? I'm terrified.
Steve	[SOFTENING] It's easier if you move.
Sonia	I'm too scared to move.
Steve	Here …
	HE OFFERS HER A HAND. SHE TAKES IT AND TEETERS TOWARDS HIM.
Sonia	Do you really do this for fun?
Steve	I'll do it for a living one day. That's my ambition.
Sonia	Sure. Like Torvill and …
	THAT'S AS FAR AS SHE GETS. HER SKATES GO OUT FROM UNDER HER AND SHE FALLS FLAT ON HER BACKSIDE. *Steve* LOOKS AT HER AND HE CAN'T HELP SMILING. AT LAST, THE ICE HAS BROKEN BETWEEN THEM (METAPHORICALLY, AT LEAST).
Sonia	All right. All right. Help me up, will you?
	Steve REACHES OUT WITH A HAND. SHE TAKES IT.
	CUT TO:

SCENE ELEVEN

Int. Police station 9.00 a.m.

> *Carrie* IS INTERVIEWING DETECTIVE SUPERINTENDENT
> *Colin Firth*. HE IS A MAN IN HIS THIRTIES, IN JACKET AND
> TIE. MORE LIKE A SMALL BUSINESSMAN THAN A
> GLAMOROUS (OR TOUGH) COP. THE SCENE IS PLAYED TO
> CAMERA, DOCUMENTARY STYLE.

Carrie   I have with me Detective Superintendent Colin Firth, who is leading the murder investigation. Detective Superintendent ...

Firth   Actually, if I can correct you, it isn't a murder investigation. Mrs Lambert is still alive.

Carrie   Yes. But if she dies ...

Firth   It still won't be murder. Not necessarily. Mrs Lambert was found unconscious at the scene of the crime. What we have to determine is, did she fall or was she pushed?

Carrie   How will you do that?

Mike   Hopefully, she'll be able to tell us herself.

Carrie   And if she fell?

Firth   Then we'd be looking at 'Burglary with Intent', Section 9/1/A of the Theft Act.

Carrie   [CAUSTIC] I hardly think that's very relevant to *her*, Detective Superintendent.

Firth   Nonetheless, that's police procedure.

Carrie   And how far *have* the police proceeded? Have you interrogated any suspects?

Firth   Again, we tend to use the word 'interview'. But the answer's, no. We're still waiting for witnesses to come forward.

Carrie   Detective Superintendent – can I take it that if Mrs Lambert dies without regaining consciousness, you will be bringing a charge of murder?

Firth   Yes. Unless she can tell us exactly what happened in that house, then we'll have no other choice.

CUT TO:

SCENE   TWELVE

Int. Maggie's hospital room 8.00 p.m.

THE *Policeman* IS WAITING. NO CHANGE IN *Maggie's* CONDITION. BUT NOW ANOTHER WOMAN WATCHES HER. THIS IS *Joyce*, HER DAUGHTER, IN HER EARLY FORTIES, PREMATURELY GREY, DEFEATED. *Karen*, IN NURSE'S UNIFORM, IS WITH HER.

Karen   I'm afraid you'll have to leave now, Miss Lambert.

Joyce   Yes, I'll come.

THEY LEAVE TOGETHER.

CUT TO:

SCENE   THIRTEEN

Int. Hospital passage 8.00 p.m.

Karen AND *Joyce* WALK TOGETHER DOWN THE CORRIDOR.

Joyce   Is there any chance? I mean, is she going to live?

Karen   You'll have to speak to the doctor. But if there's any change in her condition, we'll let you know.

THEY WALK ON A LITTLE FURTHER. *Joyce* APPEARS DISTRESSED, WITHDRAWN. *Karen* BREAKS THE SILENCE.

CUT TO: ANOTHER ANGLE.

Karen   I got to know your mother quite well, Miss Lambert. When she was in here before.

Joyce   Oh?

Karen   I know what you must be feeling.

Joyce   Do you?

Karen   It must be awful for you . . .

Joyce STOPS WALKING.

Joyce	You think so?
Karen	Well ...
Joyce	She's a horrible woman. Mean, vicious, selfish ...
Karen	[HELPLESS] I'm sorry ...
Joyce	Don't be. You don't know what it was like growing up with her. You don't know what she did to me. I've been in hospital before on her account – but not visiting. You don't know her. You don't want to know her. She's evil ...
Karen	Then why did you come?
Joyce	Why do you think? I wanted to know she'd finally gone. I wanted to see her die!

Joyce TURNS ROUND AND WALKS OUT OF THE HOSPITAL.
Karen STARES AFTER HER IN BLANK AMAZEMENT.

CUT TO:

SCENE FOURTEEN

Int. Williams' home (living room) 9.00 p.m.

Mike IS SITTING WITH *Steve*. THE TWO OF THEM ARE
WATCHING TV. THE ROOM IS FULL OF CIGARETTE SMOKE,
WHICH HANGS HEAVY IN THE AIR – AS DOES THE SILENCE
BETWEEN THEM. *Mike* IS TENSE, ON EDGE, AND *Steve* CAN
SEE THAT SOMETHING'S WRONG.

Steve	Mike?
Mike	Yeah?
Steve	You OK?
Mike	[TETCHY] Yeah.

CUT TO:

SCENE FIFTEEN

Ext. A street 9.00 a.m.

INSERT: THE TV PROGRAMME IS A COP SHOW IN THE
STYLE OF 'THE SWEENEY'. (IDEALLY, WE WOULD SHOOT

THIS OURSELVES. ALTERNATIVELY, AN EXTRACT COULD BE USED, SO LONG AS IT TIES UP WITH THE SCENE AT THE END OF THE EPISODE.) A PLAIN CLOTHES COP PURSUES A VILLAIN. DRAMATIC, POUNDING MUSIC. THE PIECE HAS FOUR (POSSIBLE) SEGMENTS.

● THE VILLAIN PUSHES DUSTBINS IN FRONT OF THE COP. THE COP JUMPS OVER THEM.

● THE VILLAIN CLIMBS A FENCE. THE COP JUST MISSES HIM, THEN FOLLOWS.

● THE VILLAIN RUNS ACROSS AN OPEN AREA. HE SHOVES ASIDE A WOMAN WHO IS PUSHING A PRAM. THE COP SWERVES TO AVOID HER.

● THE COP THROWS HIMSELF AT THE VILLAIN – A FLYING RUGBY TACKLE.

CUT TO:

SCENE SIXTEEN

Int. Williams' home (living room) 9.00 p.m.

Mike GETS UP AND TURNS THE TELEVISION SET OFF.

Steve Hey – I was watching that!

Mike I don't want to see it.

Mike LOOKS MOODILY AT HIS BROTHER, THEN MAKES FOR THE DOOR.

Steve Where are you going?

Mike Out.

Steve Where?

Mike Just out, all right?

Mike LEAVES ANGRILY. *Steve* LOOKS WORRIEDLY AT THE DOOR, THEN, AT THE OVERFLOWING ASHTRAY. HE KNOWS SOMETHING IS VERY WRONG. HE GETS UP AND LEAVES THE ROOM.

CUT TO:

SCENE SEVENTEEN ▦▦▦▦▦▦▦▦▦▦▦▦▦▦▦▦▦

Int. Williams' home (hallway) 9.00 p.m.

STILL WORRIED, *Steve* GOES UPSTAIRS. THE CAMERA
FOLLOWS HIM. HE'S GOING TO BED, BUT, AT THE TOP OF
THE STAIRS, HE PAUSES.

CUT TO: ANOTHER ANGLE. THE DOOR FACING THE STAIRS
LEADS TO *Mike's* BEDROOM. WE KNOW THIS BECAUSE
THERE'S A CHINA PLATE WITH HIS NAME ON IT. *Steve* LOOKS
BACK DOWN THE STAIRS. THERE'S NO SIGN OF *Mike.* HE
HESITATES. THEN, SOFTLY ENTERS THE ROOM.

CUT TO:

SCENE EIGHTEEN ▦▦▦▦▦▦▦▦▦▦▦▦▦▦▦▦▦

Int. Mike's bedroom 9.00 p.m.

THE ROOM IS A TIP. THE FOOTBALL POSTERS AND POP
GROUPS ON THE WALLS ARE A SAD REMINDER OF A LOST
CHILDHOOD. *Steve* POKES AROUND. AMONGST THE THINGS
HE FINDS ARE YTS LEAFLETS, A CIGARETTE PACK, FOUR
ONE-POUND COINS. HE OPENS A DRAWER, THEN ANOTHER.
RUSTLES UNDERNEATH SOME CLOTHES.

CUT TO: CLOSE SHOT. *Steve* FINDS A BOOK – A PENSION
BOOK. HE LOOKS AT IT, SLOWLY REALIZES WHAT IT IS. HE
THINKS. THEN, TAKES IT.

CUT TO:

SCENE NINETEEN ▦▦▦▦▦▦▦▦▦▦▦▦▦▦▦▦▦▦▦

Int. A police girl 9.00 p.m.

Leo IS IN A POLICE CELL WITH DETECTIVE SUPERINTENDENT
Colin Firth AND A *Policeman.* THIS SCENE IS BLEAK, BRUTAL
– NIGHTMARISH. IT IS BY FAR THE MOST VIOLENT IN THE
ENTIRE SERIES, AND THE VIOLENCE REALLY HAS TO SHOCK.
Leo HAS EVIDENTLY BEEN BEATEN UP – AND MORE THAN
ONCE. *Firth* DRAGS HIM OUT OF HIS CHAIR BY HIS THROAT.

Firth   Listen to me, you bleeding jungle bunny. I don't want any more of your nigger talk. I want the name.

Leo   [A GROAN] No ...

> CUT TO: ANOTHER ANGLE. *Firth* KNEES *Leo* SAVAGELY BETWEEN THE LEGS AND THROWS HIM ONTO THE FLOOR. BLOOD TRICKLES OUT OF *Leo's* MOUTH.

Firth   You tell me, sunshine – or you're dead.

Leo   I won't.

Firth   Oh yes, you will ...

> THE *Policeman* LAUGHS BRUTALLY, ENJOYING THE SCENE. *Firth* DRAWS BACK HIS FOOT TO KICK *Leo* IN THE HEAD.

> CUT TO:

SCENE TWENTY

Int. Leo's bedroom 9.00 p.m.

> *Leo* WAKES UP, DRENCHED IN SWEAT. THE PREVIOUS SCENE HAS BEEN A NIGHTMARE, A GROTESQUE PARODY OF HIS OWN FEARS.

> CUT TO: MONTAGE SEQUENCE. THE TV PROGRAMME AND *Leo's* NIGHTMARE HAVE GIVEN US TWO VIEWS OF THE POLICE. THIS SEQUENCE – BACKED WITH APPROPRIATE MUSIC AND FILMED IN A GRAINY DOCUMENTARY MANNER, GIVES US A THIRD.

> CUT TO:

SCENE TWENTY-ONE

Ext. A street near Maggie's house 9.00 a.m.

> CLOSE SHOT: A POLICE INCIDENT BOARD – TATTY AND FLAPPING IN THE BREEZE. THE HEADLINE IS 'DID YOU SEE?'. IT DESCRIBES TWO YOUTHS – ONE WHITE, ONE BLACK – SEEN RUNNING DOWN THE STREET.

> CUT TO:

SCENE TWENTY-TWO ░░░░░░░░░░░░░░░░░░

Ext. A housing estate 9.00 a.m.

TWO UNIFORMED *Constables* WALK ALONG THE TERRACE OF A HOUSING ESTATE, CARRYING OUT DOOR-TO-DOOR ENQUIRIES.
CAPTION 1: (IN QUOTATIONS) 'MOST OF US ARE MARRIED WITH KIDS. AND IN MANY WAYS WE'RE VERY OLD-FASHIONED.'

CUT TO: ANOTHER ANGLE. A *Constable* RINGS A DOORBELL. IT IS OPENED BY AN *Elderly man* WHO LOOKS AT HIS VISITOR WITH IMMEDIATE SUSPICION AND MISTRUST.
CAPTION 2: (IN QUOTATIONS) 'HONESTY AND TRUTHFULNESS ARE IMPORTANT TO US. SOCIETY HAS CHANGED. WE HAVEN'T. AND IN THAT WAY WE'VE FALLEN BEHIND.'

CUT TO: ANOTHER ANGLE. THE SECOND *Constable* IS RINGING ANOTHER BELL. THERE IS NO REPLY. HE IS BORED, COLD AND TIRED.

CUT TO: ANOTHER ANGLE. THE FIRST *Constable* SHOWS THE *Elderly man* A PHOTOGRAPH OF *Maggie*. HE EXPLAINS WHAT HE'S LOOKING FOR. THE *Elderly man* SHAKES HIS HEAD. HE DOESN'T WANT TO KNOW. HE SHUTS THE DOOR.
CAPTION 3: (IN QUOTATIONS) 'WE MAKE JOKES ABOUT EVERYTHING. IF WE STOPPED AND THOUGHT ABOUT WHAT'S GOING ON, WE'D BE CRYING TWENTY-FOUR HOURS A DAY.'

CUT TO: LONG SHOT. THE WHOLE HOUSING ESTATE. THE *Constables* ARE SLOWLY COVERING GROUND. THERE COULD PERHAPS BE MORE THAN TWO . . . FOUR OR FIVE?

CUT TO: ANOTHER ANGLE. GRAFFITI ON WALL: 'HELP THE POLICE. BEAT YOURSELF UP'.

CUT TO: ANOTHER ANGLE. ANOTHER DOOR OPENS. WE DON'T EVEN SEE WHOSE HOUSE IT IS. AS SOON AS THE OWNER SEES THE *Constable*, HE CLOSES IT AGAIN.

CUT TO: CAPTION 4: (IN QUOTATIONS) 'WE HAVE A WELFARE OFFICER TO LOOK AFTER 27,000 OFFICERS IN LONDON. AT ANY ONE TIME, HE HAS 400 OF THEM ON HIS BOOKS.'

CUT TO: ANOTHER ANGLE. A CONSTABLE MOVES ALONG A
TERRACE TOWARDS THE NEXT DOOR. HE HAS TO PASS A
GROUP OF BLACK YOUTHS WHO ARE HANGING AROUND
OUTSIDE. THEY LOOK ON HIM WITH RAW, NAKED
AGGRESSION. NOTHING HAPPENS, BUT IT'S A TENSE
MOMENT.

CUT TO: CAPTION 5: (IN QUOTATIONS) 'I FIND THEM VERY
DIFFICULT TO DEAL WITH BECAUSE OF THE MISTRUST
THEY HAVE. AND WHEN THEY SPEAK THE PATOIS, I CAN'T
UNDERSTAND.'

CUT TO: CAPTION 6: (IN QUOTATIONS) 'THEY'RE ALWAYS
SAYING – "YOU ONLY PICK ON ME BECAUSE I'M BLACK." I
REALLY RESENT THAT. I ONLY PICK ON THEM BECAUSE
THEY'RE CRIMINAL.'

CUT TO:

SCENE TWENTY-THREE

Int. The hospital Day

Karen IS CARRYING A TRAY OF PILLS DOWN THE CORRIDOR
PAST *Maggie's* ROOM, WHEN SHE IS SURPRISED BY *Firth*
COMING OUT, CARRYING HIS NOTEBOOK. IN THE FAINT
DISTANCE, WE CAN HEAR THE BLEEP OF THE HEART
MACHINE.

Karen Oh, hello! You're the detective . . .

Firth Colin Firth.

Karen I saw you on TV last night.

Firth [DRY] Edited highlights!

Karen Are you off, then?

Firth Yes. We got a full statement from her.

Karen Did she see the two boys?

Firth No. They'd already scarpered. She took one look at her
place, saw what they'd done and that was enough to put
her back in here.

Firth PUTS AWAY HIS NOTEBOOK.

| Firth | Anyway, it won't be murder now. Just straightforward burglary. |

Firth   Anyway, it won't be murder now. Just straightforward burglary.

Karen   Do you think you'll get them?

Firth   We've already got a positive ID on one of them. It won't be long.

Karen   Good. The little sods . . .

Firth   Sods? You think so?

Karen   Surely . . .

Firth   Kids. That's all. Probably didn't have a clue what they were doing. In a way, I feel sorry for them.

Karen   Sorry?

Firth   They broke the law. But why do people obey laws? Answer: because society rewards them for obeying the rules. But there aren't that many rewards for the kids round here, are there? Yes, I can feel sorry for them.

Karen   But you'll still catch them?

Firth   That's my job.

Karen   They could have killed her.

Firth   But they didn't, did they.?

Karen   [DOUBTFUL] So it all ends happily?

Firth   That's what we like. Happy endings.

THE WORDS ARE NO SOONER SPOKEN THAN THERE IS A SUDDEN, SHRILL SCREAM FROM THE HEART MACHINE . . . A SOUND THAT EVERYONE KNOWS. *Maggie's* HEART HAS STOPPED BEATING. *Karen* FREEZES FOR A SECOND. THEN, SHE RUSHES INTO THE ROOM, FOLLOWED BY *Firth*. OTHER HOSPITAL STAFF FOLLOW.

CUT TO:

SCENE TWENTY-FOUR

Ext. Maggie's house 12.00 p.m.

AS IN ELEVEN, *Carrie* IS INTERVIEWING *Joyce* FOR HER NEWS

PROGRAMME.

Joyce You want me to tell you something about my mother?

Carrie If it's not too painful.

Joyce It is painful. Very painful. But not in the way you think. I'm sorry, Miss Andrews – but I don't think I can help you with your programme.

Carrie Just tell me in your own words.

Joyce I remember her so well. She was a strong woman, once. And she drank. If me or my brother upset her – if we made a mess, if we cried – she had a metal rod and she used it on us. Once, she broke my arm. Then, at the hospital, she made me tell them that I'd had a fall . . .

Carrie Where was your father?

Joyce I never knew him. After I left, she lived alone. I went to see her sometimes. I don't know why.

Carrie How did you feel about her death?

Joyce What those two boys did to her – nobody can forgive them for that. But I don't think they meant to do it. And . . . I'm sorry, I know it's a terrible thing to say, but I cannot find it in my heart to forgive her, for what she did to me. People like my mother . . . they're animals.

CUT TO:

SCENE   TWENTY-FIVE

Ext. A breaker's yard 7.00 p.m.

A COUPLE OF OLD TV SETS ARE PROMINENT AMIDST THE GENERAL RUBBLE. FRIGHTENED AND ON THE RUN, *Mike* AND *Leo* MEET FOR A LAST TIME. THE DESOLATION OF THE BREAKER'S YARD SOMEHOW REFLECTS THE HOPELESSNESS OF THEIR SITUATION.

Mike You heard?

Leo Yeah. I heard it on the news.

Mike She's dead, Leo.

Leo Yeah. But we didn't kill her. She never even saw us.

Mike They'll never believe that.

Leo They got to find us first ...

Mike They'll find us. In time ...

A LONG PAUSE. A COLD WIND BLOWS THROUGH THE
BREAKER'S YARD.

Mike Leo – how did we get here?

Leo On the bus.

Mike No, I mean – here. You and me. We didn't want to hurt
anyone. I didn't. You didn't. When we broke into the
house, it was just a game – wasn't it.

Leo Sure. [PAUSE] Of course, there was the money ...

Mike No. It wasn't the money. I only ever felt human when I
was with you. All those things we did, TDA*. Bunking
out of restaurants. That was *me*. That was my choice.

Leo I don't get you, Mike ...

Mike I thought I'd found myself with you. But then, I look in
the papers. I see that woman on TV. And it isn't me.
She's talking about someone else.

Leo If the pigs find someone else, that's fine by me.

Mike Oh, Leo ...

Mike AND *Leo* CLUTCH HANDS IN A GESTURE OF
FRIENDSHIP AND SOLIDARITY.

CUT TO:

*Talking and Drinking Away.

SCENE TWENTY-SIX

Ext. Outside a McDonalds 7.00 p.m.

Sonia AND *Steve* MEET, AS ARRANGED.

Sonia Are you going to buy me a hamburger, then?

Steve Can I talk to you?

Sonia	I'm here, aren't I?
Steve	But you must promise. You won't tell. Not anyone.
Sonia	What have you done?
Steve	I haven't done anything.
Sonia	Go on, then.
Steve	Look – suppose you had a really close friend and you found he'd done something. Something really terrible. What would you do?
Sonia	Well, it depends ...
Steve	Suppose he'd killed someone?
Sonia	Steve !

A PAUSE. *Steve* MAKES UP HIS MIND. HE PRODUCES THE BOOK HE FOUND IN *Mike's* ROOM AND GIVES IT TO *Sonia*.

Steve	Here.
Sonia	What is it?
Steve	It's a pension book.

Sonia READS THE NAME ON THE FRONT.

Sonia	'Maggie Lambert.' Wasn't she ...
Steve	Yeah.
Sonia	Where'd you get this?
Steve	I found it. In Mike's bedroom. You won't tell anyone!
Sonia	I said I wouldn't. Mike's bedroom. Mike ... your brother?
Steve	Yeah.
Sonia	Where do you think he got it?
Steve	Where do you think?

Sonia REALISES.

Sonia	So what are you going to do?
Steve	That's what I'm asking you. What do I do?
Sonia	You could go to the police.
Steve	I can't!

Sonia	You've got to. I mean, what he did . . . it's awful.
Steve	He's still my brother.
Sonia	I thought you were adopted.
Steve	Same difference.

ANOTHER PAUSE.

Sonia	I wish you hadn't told me.
Steve	I had to tell someone.
Sonia	Yeah. Well, you know what this makes you? It makes you an accessory. That's what it's called. And now you've told me, so I am, too.

Sonia LOOKS DOWN AT THE PENSION BOOK WITH DREAD.

CUT TO:

SCENE TWENTY-SEVEN

Int. Outside Williams' house 8.00 p.m.

Steve RETURNS TO THE HOUSE ALONE, THOUGHTFUL. AS HE REACHES THE DRIVE, WHERE THE DUSTBINS STAND, *Karen* COMES OUT, ON HER WAY TO HER CAR.

Karen	Steve! I thought I'd miss you.
Steve	Hi, Karen.
Karen	You sound down in the dumps. You and Mike both.
Steve	I've just been thinking . . .

A PAUSE.

Steve	You knew that old woman, didn't you?
Karen	Who?
Steve	The one who got killed.
Karen	Yes. But don't waste any tears over her. It seems she wasn't quite the saint everyone's making her out to be.
Steve	What?
Karen	I met the daughter. According to her, 'Old Maggie'

	deserved everything she got.
Steve	She said that?
Karen	And more besides.
Steve	That's not what it said on the telly.
Karen	Well, you shouldn't believe everything you see on TV.
Steve	She's still dead.
Karen	I know. But that doesn't make any difference. Whenever anyone dies, it's always the same. You always have to feel sorry for them – even a monster like Mrs Lambert. Dying is like going into a washing-machine. All the bad things get rinsed out.

Karen MOVES TOWARDS THE CAR.

Karen	Anyway – I've got to dash. I'm on night shift. See you.
Steve	Yeah. See you.

Karen GETS INTO HER CAR. *Steve* WATCHES HER AS SHE STARTS THE ENGINE AND DRIVES AWAY. THEN HE TAKES OUT THE PENSION BOOK. HE LOOKS AT IT. THEN, OPENS A DUSTBIN AND STUFFS IT DEEP INSIDE.

CUT TO:

SCENE TWENTY-EIGHT

Int. Police station (interrogation room) 9.00 a.m.

Firth IS SITTING OPPOSITE *Leo*. THE SAME CELL AND THE SAME MAN AS IN *Leo's* NIGHTMARE. BUT THE REALITY IS DIFFERENT.

Firth	Cigarette?

Leo SHAKES HIS HEAD.

Firth	Look, Leo. You've got to be sensible. I want the name.

A LONG PAUSE.

Firth	Who went in there with you? The other lad. There's no point protecting him. We'll get him anyway, in the end.

ANOTHER PAUSE. BUT *Leo* IS MASTER OF THE SITUATION.

100

Firth   You're just going to make things worse for yourself. Can't you see that?

ANOTHER PAUSE.

Firth   OK, have it your way. Your brief's outside. I suggest you talk it over with him.

Leo SMILES. HE HASN'T GIVEN *Mike* AWAY. AND HE HASN'T BEEN BEATEN UP.

CUT TO:

SCENE TWENTY-NINE

Int. Cutting room 9.00 a.m.

THE SCREENS OF THE STEINBECK INTRODUCE THE FINAL SEQUENCE OF THE PLAY, WHICH SHOULD BE UNIFIED, ALMOST WITH A MONTAGE EFFECT. MUSIC THROUGHOUT? THE SCREENS SHOW *Maggie's* FUNERAL PROCESSION, HER FUNERAL, *Carrie* TALKING INTO A MIKE AND *Joyce's* INTERVIEW.

Producer   [v/o] And, action!

CUT TO:

SCENE THIRTY

Ext. A cemetery 11.00 a.m.

Carrie IS DISCREETLY ON THE EDGE OF THE CEMETERY, TALKING TO CAMERA.

Carrie   Today they are burying old Maggie Lambert, the victim of a brutal and cowardly assault. In the midst of all the grief, questions cry out to be answered.

CUT TO:

SCENE THIRTY-ONE ░░░░░░░░░░░░░░░░░░░░░░░░

Ext. Approach to cemetery 11.00 a.m.

THE HEARSE CARRYING *Maggie's* COFFIN APPROACHES THE CEMETERY.

Carrie [v/o] Where are the police when we most need them? Why must crime and violence run riot in our streets?

CUT TO:

SCENE THIRTY-TWO ░░░░░░░░░░░░░░░░░░░░░░░░

Ext. Mike's bedroom 11.00 a.m.

Mike LOOKING UP OUT OF THE WINDOW – ALONE, AFRAID.

Carrie [v/o] And must old people live their lives in fear? Is there nothing we can do to stop the thugs who prey on them?

CUT TO:

SCENE THIRTY-THREE ░░░░░░░░░░░░░░░░░░░░░░░░

Insert THIS IS AN EDITED CLIP OF THE INTERVIEW BETWEEN *Carrie* AND *Joyce* (SCENE TWENTY-FOUR). THE UNDERLINED PASSAGES IN THAT SCENE HAVE BEEN CUT TOGETHER TO GIVE A COMPLETELY NEW MEANING.

Joyce It is painful. Very painful.

Carrie Just tell me in your own words.

Joyce I remember her so well. She was a strong woman, once. After I left, she lived alone. I went to see her sometimes ...

Carrie How did you feel about her death?

Joyce What those two boys did to her – nobody can forgive them for that. I'm sorry, I know it's a terrible thing to say. But I cannot find it in my heart to forgive. They're animals.

CUT TO:

SCENE THIRTY-FOUR ▦▦▦▦▦▦▦▦▦▦▦▦
Ext. Approach to cemetery 11.00 a.m.

Carrie   [v/o] What punishment can we find for the vicious animals who extinguished a life and left behind so much grief?

CUT TO:

SCENE THIRTY-FIVE ▦▦▦▦▦▦▦▦▦▦▦▦
Int. Steve's school (headmaster's study) 11.00 a.m.

Sonia   I wasn't going to tell, sir. I mean, I promised. But then when I saw on TV – you know, the daughter. Well . . . I had to.

Headmaster   Quite right, Sonia. You did the right thing. Now, if you'll excuse me . . .

THE *Headmaster* REACHES FOR THE TELEPHONE.

CUT TO:

SCENE THIRTY-SIX ▦▦▦▦▦▦▦▦▦▦▦▦
Ext. Cemetery 11.00 a.m.

THE COFFIN IS CARRIED TOWARDS THE OPEN GRAVE. THERE MAY HAVE BEEN MUSIC ON THE SOUNDTRACK THROUGHOUT THESE MONTAGE SCENES. NOW IT SWELLS UP – PERHAPS SOLO ORGAN IN FULL BLAST.

CUT TO:

SCENE THIRTY-SEVEN ▦▦▦▦▦▦▦▦▦▦▦▦
Ext. Williams' home 11.00 a.m.

A POLICE CAR SCREECHES TO A HALT OUTSIDE THE HOUSE.

Firth GETS OUT. ALL THE ANGLES AND THE ACTION IN
THESE 'ARREST' SEQUENCES ARE STRAIGHT OUT OF A TV
COP DRAMA, A DELIBERATE PARODY.

CUT TO:

SCENE THIRTY-EIGHT

Ext. Cemetery 11.00 a.m.

THE COFFIN IS CARRIED FORWARD. A *Vicar* BEGINS THE
USUAL FUNERAL ORATION. IT IS POSSIBLE THAT WE DON'T
EVEN HEAR THE WORDS.

CUT TO:

SCENE THIRTY-NINE

Ext. A street 11.00 a.m.

THIS IS AN EXACT COPY OF THE 'SWEENEY' PROGRAMME IN
SCENE FIFTEEN. ONLY THIS TIME, *Mike* IS THE VILLAIN AND
Firth IS THE COP. *Mike*'S ON THE RUN. HE TIPS DUSTBINS
OVER TO ESCAPE FROM *Firth*. *Firth* JUMPS OVER THEM.

CUT TO:

SCENE FORTY

Ext. Cemetery 11.00 a.m.

CLOSE SHOT: ON THE *Vicar* DRONING ON.

CUT TO:

SCENE FORTY-ONE

Ext. A street 11.00 a.m.

THE PARODY CONTINUES. *Mike* SCRAMBLES OVER A FENCE.

Firth JUST MISSES HIM, THEN FOLLOWS.

CUT TO:

SCENE FORTY-TWO
Ext. Cemetery 11.00 a.m.

Joyce PLAYS HER PART – THE GRIEVING DAUGHTER. THE HYPOCRISY OF TV AND THE HYPOCRISY OF FUNERALS ARE FOR A MOMENT PERFECTLY ALIGNED.

CUT TO:

SCENE FORTY-THREE
Ext. A street 11.00 a.m.

THE THIRD SEQUENCE IN THE PARODY. *Mike* ALMOST KNOCKS A *Woman pushing a pram* OVER. *Firth* SWERVES TO AVOID HER.

CUT TO:

SCENE FORTY-FOUR
Ext. Cemetery 11.00 a.m.

Karen IS ALSO AMONGST THE MOURNERS. SHE GLANCES AT *Joyce*. SHE KNOWS THE TRUTH – *Joyce* IS ACTING. THE WHOLE THING IS AN ELABORATE CHARADE.

CUT TO:

SCENE FORTY-FIVE
Ext. A street 11.00 a.m.

THE LAST PART OF THE ARREST SEQUENCE *Mike* FLEES ACROSS OPEN GROUND. *Firth* THROWS HIMSELF AT HIM IN A PERFECT RUGBY TACKLE. *Mike* COMES CRASHING DOWN TO

THE GROUND.

Firth You're nicked!

CUT TO:

SCENE   FORTY-SIX   ▦▦▦▦▦▦▦▦▦▦▦▦▦▦▦▦▦▦▦▦

Ext. Cemetery 11.00 a.m.

Karen REALISES SHE SHOULD NEVER HAVE COME. IN MID-FUNERAL, SHE WALKS AWAY, LEAVING THE SHAM BEHIND HER.

CUT TO: BLACKOUT.

CUT TO: END CREDITS.

Judgements

CHARACTERS

John Williams
Sally Williams
Mike Williams
Steve Williams
Karen Williams
Leo Young
Frances Young
Sonia
Derek
Magistrate
Producer

SCENE ONE ░░░░░░░░░░░░░░░░░░░░░░░░░░░░░░░

Int. Magistrate's court 10.00 a.m.

THE MOMENT OF JUDGEMENT. *Mike* IS BACK IN FRONT OF THE *Magistrate*. TRAPPED IN THE DARKNESS THAT SURROUNDS HIM.

Magistrate Michael Williams. You broke into an elderly woman's house with the intent to steal money you could find. As a result of your actions, the woman had a heart attack and died.

CUT TO: CLOSE SHOT ON *Mike*. HE IS DRAWN, PALE, WAITING FOR THE VERDICT.

Magistrate You can count yourself lucky not to be facing a charge of murder.

CUT TO: RESUME ON *Magistrate*.

Magistrate Nonetheless, this was a serious crime and one which should carry a custodial sentence. And it is now my duty to pass sentence on you.

CUT TO:

SCENE TWO ░░░░░░░░░░░░░░░░░░░░░░░░░░░░░░░

Opening credits.

CUT TO:

SCENE THREE ░░░░░░░░░░░░░░░░░░░░░░░░░░░░

Caption and comment montage

CAPTION ONE: 'IN 1973, 17,000 TEENAGERS WERE SENTENCED TO JAIL IN THE UK.'
COMMENT ONE: *John*, FILMED IN A DOCUMENTARY MANNER, TALKS DIRECT TO CAMERA.

John People say the parents are to blame. Or they say that society is to blame. Why is it that nobody ever says the kids are to blame?

CAPTION TWO: 'IN 1983, 30,000 TEENAGERS WERE SENTENCED TO JAIL IN THE UK'.

COMMENT TWO: *Sonia* AND *Derek* ARE TALKING IN THE SCHOOL CORRIDOR.

Derek   They ought to hang him.

Sonia   What good's that gonna do?

Derek   Well – it's a punishment, isn't it?

Sonia   Are you always this stupid, Derek, or have you been practising?

CAPTION THREE: 'BRITAIN LOCKS UP MORE TEENAGERS THAN ANY EUROPEAN COUNTRY'.

COMMENT THREE: *Karen* INTERVIEWED AT THE HOSPITAL.

Karen   What do these magistrates know, anyway? They're in their comfortable lives. They don't know what it's like to be young, or to be poor, or to be out of work. What right have they got to judge?

CAPTION FOUR: 'EIGHTY PER CENT OF PRISONERS RE-OFFEND'.

CUT TO:

SCENE FOUR ▨▨▨▨▨▨▨▨▨▨▨▨▨▨▨▨▨▨▨▨▨▨▨▨▨▨▨▨▨▨

Int. Magistrate's court 10.05 a.m.

EXACTLY THE SAME AS SCENE ONE. A FEW SECONDS HAVE PASSED.

Magistrate   I have given your case a lot of thought. Your background. Your respectable family and the fact that you haven't been in trouble before. Nonetheless, I must also take into account the very proper public outrage at offences like this.

A BRIEF PAUSE.

Magistrate   I am sentencing you to six months youth custody. And I only hope it will be a lesson to you for the future.

CUT TO: REACTION ON *Mike*. HE CANNOT BELIEVE WHAT

HE HAS JUST HEARD.

CUT TO:

SCENE FIVE ░░░░░░░░░░░░░░░░░░░░░░░░░░░░░░░░

Int. Police station (visiting room) 3.00 p.m.

Leo IS BEING VISITED BY HIS MOTHER, *Frances*, WHOM WE LAST SAW IN *It's Never Black and White*.

Leo   It's not fair.

Frances   What isn't fair, Leo?

Leo   We did it together. It was his idea. Six months!

Frances   They were tough on him.

Leo   Yeah. And what do you think they're gonna give me? Six years, more like.

Leo LIGHTS A CIGARETTE.

Frances   When did you start smoking?

Leo HOLDS OUT THE CIGARETTE WITHOUT ACTUALLY SMOKING IT.

Leo   When I lit the cigarette.

Frances   You want a death sentence?

Leo JABS FORWARD WITH THE CIGARETTE.

Leo   Six months is nothing. That's white justice. One law for him, one law for me.

Frances   His case has got nothing to do with you.

Leo   Oh, yeah?

Frances   I've spoken to your solicitor. You've been 'severed' – that's what they call it. Two cases. Two trials. Two people.

Leo   Well, that's very convenient, isn't it?

Frances   Leo, if they flogged Mike – or hanged him, would it make you feel any better?

Leo   It might.

Frances	I thought he was your friend? Or maybe that got 'severed' along the way, too?
Leo	Look, mum. *I'm* the one in this mess. And don't tell me that he got off because the judge liked his eyes or because he was only sixteen or because he's promised to be a good boy from now on. He got off because he's white. That's it – pure and simple. And if I was white I'd have got a job, I'd have a house and I wouldn't be going down for something I didn't even do.

A PAUSE.

Frances	You're not going down, Leo.
Leo	Says who?
Frances	Your solicitor. I've had a long talk with him.
Leo	Yeah?
Frances	To start with, you're going to get bail.

BEFORE *Leo* CAN INTERRUPT.

Frances	Don't worry. That's my money. My savings.
Leo	What then?
Frances	Then? We fight it. Your solicitor thinks there's a good chance he can get you off the hook.
Leo	[CYNICAL] Sure, mother.
Frances	[EXASPERATED] At least he's going to try! I'm going to try! But when are you going to start trying, Leo?

ANOTHER PAUSE. *Leo* IS SLIGHTLY TAKEN ABACK BY THE PASSION IN *Frances'* VOICE.

Frances	Sure – we've never had it easy in this country, Leo. But it's not going to change. Not until we get our act together and show them we're as good as they are. We can become rich. We can become powerful. But we can never become white. So we've got to find the answer in ourselves. We've got to forget all that black–white stuff. If *we* don't, *they* never will. Hey, give me a cigarette.

Leo GIVES *Frances* A CIGARETTE. SHE LIGHTS IT.

Frances	I haven't smoked for twelve years. That's how angry you make me.

111

Leo	Suppose I do get out of here . . .
Frances	You will get out of here.
Leo	What then?
Frances	I don't know, Leo. But you've got so much talent in you – that's what matters. And talent doesn't have a colour.

Frances COUGHS ON THE CIGARETTE.

Frances	Hey – what are these?

Leo SHOWS HER THE PACKET.

Leo	Rothmans.
Frances	South African tobacco?

Frances STUBS OUT HER CIGARETTE. *Leo* SMILES AND DOES THE SAME.

CUT TO:

SCENE SIX

Int. Williams' home 10.30 p.m.

Sally AND *John* ARE IN BED. IT IS THE NIGHT AFTER THE TRIAL. JOHN IS STARING INTO NOTHING. SALLY IS READING A BOOK

John	I still don't believe it.
Sally	What?
John	Mike.
Sally	It's only six months, John.
John	That's not what I mean. I mean, that's exactly what I mean. Six months. It's a joke, isn't it?
Sally	I didn't see Mike laughing.
John	He and that other kid. They killed someone, Sally. Maybe they didn't put a gun to her head. But it was the same in the end.
Sally	You wanted him to get more?
John	You just look at the streets out there. What happened to

law and order – eh? You tell me that. Law and order! They treat kids with cotton gloves these days. If we'd been a bit tougher with Mike this might never have happened.

Sally   I don't believe this.

John   I didn't believe it.

Sally   No, I mean you. Do you know who you're talking about? Mike? You remember? Your son?

John   My adopted son.

Sally   Oh – well, that's it. Your adopted son. You never let him forget that, did you?

John   He never let me forget it.

Sally   And did you ever talk to him about it? Really talk? Did you ever think what it might mean to him?

John   I looked after him. I gave him a good home.

Sally   Well, obviously a good home wasn't enough.

SCENE SEVEN

Ext. Steve's school (grounds) 11.00 a.m.

THE USUAL ASSORTMENT OF KIDS IN THE GROUNDS. *Derek* (SURROUNDED BY A GANG OF HIS CRONIES) IS LOOKING FOR *Sonia*. HE FINDS HER.

Derek   Sonia ...

Sonia   What do you want, Derek?

Derek   I hear you've taken up ice-skating.

Sonia   Who says?

Derek   You and Steve Williams ...

Sonia   What if I have?

Derek   Fancy yourself, do you? Torville and Dean of the Lower Fifth?

Sonia   Very funny, Derek, I don't think.

Sonia IS.ABOUT.TO MOVE OFF, BUT *Derek* STOPS HER.

Derek   Got a soft spot for poofs then, have you?

Sonia   He's not a poof, Derek.

Derek   You given him one, then?

Sonia   Get lost!

Derek   You're wasting your time, Sonia. He's a poof. A gay boy. I'd wear rubber gloves if I went skating with him.

ONE OF THE GANG NUDGES *Derek.* HE LOOKS ACROSS THE GROUNDS.

CUT TO: ANOTHER ANGLE. *Steve* HAS APPEARED. *Derek* CALLS OUT TO HIM.

Derek   Hey – Steve!

WARILY, *Steve* APPROACHES.

Derek   I heard about your brother.

Steve   What about it?

Derek   I just wondered what it must be like to have a big brother in jail.

Sonia   Why don't you leave off, Derek?

Derek   Knocked off an old lady, did he? I hear he . . . fiddled with her, too.

Steve   That's not true.

Derek   That's what I heard. Him and the other guy. They gave her one.

Sonia   You really are filthy, Derek. You know that?

Derek   I'm talking to the boyfriend, Sonia. Of course, if he wants to hide behind your skirt . . .

Steve   [QUIETLY] Derek, why don't you naff off?

Steve HAS NEVER REACTED THIS WAY BEFORE. WHAT FOLLOWS UNDERLINES THE CHANGE.

Derek   What?

Steve   Mike didn't kill anybody. He got into trouble, that's all. And if you weren't such a plonker, you'd see it wasn't anything to laugh about.

Derek	What did you call me?
Sonia	[WORRIED] Steve . . .
Steve	[TO *Derek*] YOU HEARD.
Derek	You want to come here and say that?
Steve	Sure.

Steve STEPS FORWARD. *Derek* IS TALLER THAN HIM AND A LOT HEAVIER.

Steve	Go and play with yourself somewhere else. If anyone should be in prison, it's cretins like you. Only you'd probably get a kick out of it.
Derek	Why you . . .

Derek MOVES FORWARD TO PUNCH *Steve*. BUT *Sonia* STOPS HIM.

Sonia	Not here, Derek.
Derek	You're just scared for him.
Sonia	Scared for him? Why should I be scared for him. He's only half your size.

Derek LOOKS AROUND HIM. HE SEES THAT THERE ARE TEACHERS ABOUT.

Derek	All right, then – where?

Sonia LOOKS FROM *Derek* TO *Steve*. LIKE ANY SCHOOL BULLY, *Derek* IS QUIETLY CONFIDENT. AFTER ALL, HE'S SEVERAL INCHES TALLER AND SEVERAL POUNDS HEAVIER THAN HIS OPPONENT.

Steve	You name the time. I'll say the place.
Derek	[MOCKING] Sure. Time – fifty years from now. Place – anywhere I'm not.
Steve	Go on.
Derek	All right, then. Five o'clock this afternoon. That suit you?
Steve	Five o'clock.
Derek	And the place?

A PAUSE. ALL EYES ARE ON *Steve* AND *Sonia* IS WORRIED. IT LOOKS LIKE HE'S GOING TO GET A THRASHING.

Steve	At the rink.

Steve HAS TURNED THE TABLES.

Derek	Wait a minute . . .
Steve	On the ice.
Derek	That's crazy.
Sonia	You agreed, Derek. You said the time. He says the place.
Derek	But that's not . . .
Sonia	What's wrong? You can skate, can't you?
Derek	Yeah, but . . .
Sonia	You're bigger than he is. It makes it fairer.

Derek LOOKS FOR SUPPORT FROM HIS MATES, BUT THEY LIKE THE IDEA OF AN ICE FIGHT. HE REALISES THERE'S NO WAY OUT.

Derek	All right. I can beat you anywhere . . .

Derek TURNS ROUND AND MARCHES OFF.

CUT TO:

SCENE EIGHT ▦▦▦▦▦▦▦▦▦▦▦▦▦▦▦▦▦▦▦▦▦▦▦

Ext. Street near Leo's flat 5.00 p.m.

Mike HAS MANAGED TO BREAK OUT OF DETENTION. HE GETS OFF A BUS AND SLIPS THROUGH THE STREETS, ON THE RUN, AFRAID OF BEING SEEN. HIS PRISON UNIFORM IS DISGUISED BY A SHABBY COAT.

CUT TO:

SCENE NINE ▦▦▦▦▦▦▦▦▦▦▦▦▦▦▦▦▦▦▦▦▦▦▦

Int. Corridor outside Leo's flat 5.10 p.m.

Leo OPENS THE DOOR TO FIND *Mike* WAITING THERE.

Leo	Mike . . .

Mike	Let me in, Leo.
Leo	Wait ...
Mike	Let me in, OK?

Mike PUSHES PAST AND GOES IN.

CUT TO:

SCENE TEN

Int. Leo's flat (living room) 5.15 p.m.

Frances IS THERE, CLEANING. SHE SEES *Mike* COME IN, WITH *Leo* CLOSE BEHIND.

Frances	You're Mike. Mike Williams. What are you doing here?

AN AWKWARD PAUSE.

Frances	You've broken out, haven't you!
Mike	Yes.
Frances	How?
Mike	It wasn't exactly Alcatraz.
Frances	Why have you come here?
Mike	To see Leo.
Leo	It's OK, mum.
Frances	It is *not* OK. It is *not* OK. [TO *Mike*] Do you know what will happen if the police find you here?
Mike	To me?
Frances	No. Not to you. To Leo. [PAUSE] He's on bail. He's got his own trial in two weeks.
Leo	Mum, please ...
Frances	Haven't you got Leo in enough trouble? Why can't you leave us alone?
Mike	I just want to talk to him.
Frances	I don't believe this!
Mike	Just five minutes. Then I'll go.

Leo   Mum ...

Frances   [TO *Leo*] YOU'LL NEVER LEARN, WILL YOU?

Leo   He just wants to talk. And he's here now. It can't hurt.

> A PAUSE.

Frances   [TO *Mike*] Five minutes. Then I call the police.

> *Frances* LEAVES THE ROOM. *Leo* AND *Mike* LOOK AT EACH
> OTHER. *Mike* SLUMPS INTO A CHAIR.

Mike   Not exactly Mr Popular, am I?

Leo   You OK, Mike?

Mike   Yeah. I'm OK.

Leo   Why have you come here? You're crazy!

> *Mike* SHRUGS.

Mike   Got a drink?

Leo   No.

Mike   Thanks.

> A PAUSE.

Leo   So, what's doing?

Mike   I'm getting out of the country.

Leo   What?

Mike   I met a guy inside. He told me. There's a way ...

Leo   No passport? No money?

Mike   There are ways, Leo.

Leo   Two weeks youth custody and you sound like something out of a TV film. So you're going abroad?

Mike   I want you to come with me.

Leo   Me? And what do we do when we get there?

Mike   We'll be OK. You don't want to go inside, Leo ...

Leo   No, but I'm out on bail. My mum had to pay. All her savings – and more.

Mike   You can pay her back – one day. I've got it all planned. You and me. We start in Ireland. We get a ship across from ...

Leo   [INTERRUPTING] Mike. Mike! I'm not going anywhere.

Mike   What?

Leo   I'm not going anywhere, Mike. Not with you.

Mike   You know where you're going if you hang around here?

Leo   Maybe. But you must have a screw loose if you think I'm gonna slip on board some ship to Ireland with you ...

Mike   Leo. You and me ...

Leo   That's finished, Mike. What we did – it was stupid. Unnecessary.

Mike   What are you saying?

Leo   I'm saying the truth, man! Can't you see that? We were just kids. Wasting time.

Mike   We fought the system.

Leo   We fought nothing. Breaking into that old woman's house. That was just stupid. What did we think we were going to find? What were we going to do with it if we did find it? We were fooling ourselves. Only I was too stupid to see it.

Mike   Leo ...

Leo   No, Mike. I've had time to think things through. You know? And I think that I'm better than that. Better than I was with you.

Mike   [BITTER] Is that what you are going to tell the judge?

Leo   I'm my own judge. Look, Mike, I like you. But we did one hell of a bad thing together. And I really don't want to see you again. I'm sorry, but that's how it is.

Mike GETS UP.

Mike   Yeah. Sure.

Leo   Come on, Mike. You got to grow up some time. Six months, you'll be out. You can start again – leave all this behind.

Mike   Sure. I'll see you, Leo.

Mike MOVES TO THE DOOR. THEN PAUSES.

Mike	Your mum. Will she call the police?
Leo	No, Mike. You will.
Mike	Yeah.

Mike LEAVES.

CUT TO:

SCENE ELEVEN
Ext. Williams' home 7.00 p.m.

John IS STANDING OUTSIDE, LOOKING OUT INTO THE ROAD. *Sally* JOINS HIM.

Sally	Karen gone?
John	Yes.
Sally	You're looking for Mike?
John	Yes.
Sally	You really think he'll come here?
John	Where else can he go?
Sally	He knows how you feel about him, John. He knows how you've judged him. I don't think he'll come here.

Sally TURNS AND GOES BACK INTO THE HOUSE. *John* IS LEFT OUT IN THE COLD.

CUT TO:

SCENE TWELVE
Int. The ice rink 7.30 p.m.

THE RINK IS EMPTY – ABOUT TO CLOSE FOR THE EVENING. ONLY *Steve* AND *Derek* ARE ON THE ICE. ONE CAMP (*Derek's* SUPPORTERS) IS ON THE STAND NEXT TO HIM. *Sonia* IS WITH *Steve* AT THE OTHER END.

Sonia	You don't need to do this, Steve.
Steve	Yes, I do.

Sonia   Why? You've got nothing to prove. Not to me, anyway.

Steve   It's not you, Sonia. It's me. I'm fed up with being judged by the likes of Derek and his lot. Fed up.

Sonia   If he gets anywhere near you, he'll murder you.

Steve   He won't get anywhere near me.

CUT TO: ANOTHER ANGLE. *Derek* SKATES TOWARDS *Steve*. SURPRISINGLY, HE'S QUITE ACCOMPLISHED ON ICE.

Derek   Come on, pretty boy.

Derek TURNS AND SKATES OUT.

CUT TO: ANOTHER ANGLE. THE FIGHT. IT'S A FIST FIGHT. THE FIRST PERSON TO GRAB THE OTHER ONE WILL BE THE LIKELY WINNER. THE VARIOUS SUPPORTERS CHEER THEIR MAN ON. BUT ALTHOUGH *Derek* CAN MOVE ABOUT, *Steve* LITERALLY WEAVES CIRCLES ROUND HIM. IT'S ANOTHER BRAVURA PERFORMANCE, DEMONSTRATING HIS COMPLETE MASTERY.

IT ENDS AS HE COMES SPIRALLING IN FOR ANOTHER CLOSE PASS. *Derek* LUNGES OUT TO GRAB HIM, LOSES HIS BALANCE AND FALLS FLAT ON HIS BACK. *Steve* IS ALREADY MOVING AWAY FAST, BUT SUDDENLY, HE SPINS ROUND, THEN COMES SHOOTING BACK.

CUT TO: LOW ANGLE. THE CAMERA IS ON THE GROUND WITH *Derek*. SUDDENLY, HE IS AFRAID, AND FROM THIS ANGLE WE CAN SEE WHY. *Steve*'S SKATES, RAZOR SHARP, ARE BEARING DOWN ON HIS NECK. IT LOOKS AS IF HE'S GOING TO DECAPITATE *Derek*.

BUT, AT THE LAST MOMENT, HE COMES TO A PERFECTLY TIMED AND IMPRESSIVE STOP. HE'S RIGHT ABOVE *Derek* NOW. HE RAISES ONE FOOT. THE BLADE RESTS ACROSS *Derek's* THROAT.

Derek   [WHIMPERING] No, please ...

Steve   Just get off my back, Derek.

CUT TO: ANOTHER ANGLE. *Steve* TURNS AND SKATES AWAY. *Derek's* CREDIBILITY HAS BEEN SHATTERED, AT LEAST FOR THE TIME BEING. AND *Steve*, IN A WAY, HAS FOUND HIMSELF.

FADE TO BLACK – HOLD THEN ...

CUT TO:

SCENE THIRTEEN ▨▨▨▨▨▨▨▨▨▨▨▨▨▨▨▨▨▨▨

Ext. A station 12.00 midday

Mike COMES OUT OF A RAILWAY STATION, DRESSED IN THE SAME CLOTHES THAT HE WORE IN THE COURTROOM AND CARRYING A BAG. HE IS SURPRISED TO FIND *John* WAITING FOR HIM.

John Hello, Mike. You OK?

Mike Yeah. I'm OK.

John You've lost weight.

Mike A bit. [PAUSE] I thought Karen was coming for me.

John She was. But I said I would.

Mike NOTICES THE CAR.

Mike You've got a new car.

John Yeah.

Mike Nice.

John It's all right. [PAUSE] You want to get in then?

Mike Sure.

THIS CLIPPED, AWKWARD CONVERSATION UNDERLINES THE UNEASINESS BETWEEN FATHER AND SON. *Mike* AND *John* MOVE TO THE CAR.

CUT TO:

SCENE FOURTEEN ▨▨▨▨▨▨▨▨▨▨▨▨▨▨▨▨▨▨▨

Int./Ext. John's car 12.15 p.m.

John AND *Mike* DRIVE HOME.

John So when do you get to see your probation officer?

Mike Tomorrow.

John	And then?
Mike	I don't know.
John	But you're OK?
Mike	Yeah. I'm OK.

SILENCE. THEY DRIVE ON FOR A WHILE.

John	Look, Mike. I came for you, because I wanted to say something.
Mike	Leave it out, dad ...
John	No. I just want you to know ... I mean, I've been thinking about things. Talking. And maybe I could have been more help. You know. All that time you were living in my house ... but I never really knew you.
Mike	Dad ...
John	I guess a lot of parents don't know their kids. They just take them for granted. Or worse, they try to turn them into what they want them to be. Well, that's all right for most of them. But you ... you're different. So, I'm sorry, right?
Mike	Sure, dad.
John	All I'm saying is, Mike. Just – you know, bear with me. Now that you're back. I want this to work. I want *us* to work.
Mike	Just get me home, dad. I'm starved.

Mike AND *John* DRIVE ON. THE DELIVERY OF THE CONVERSATION SHOULD LEAVE *Mike's* FUTURE AND HIS RELATIONSHIP WITH *John* AN OPEN QUESTION.

CUT TO:

SCENE FIFTEEN

Ext. Williams' home 12.45 p.m.

ESTABLISHING SHOT: THE CAR IS PARKED OUTSIDE.

CUT TO:

SCENE SIXTEEN ████████████████████████████████

Int. Williams' home (dining room) 1.00 p.m.

CLOSE SHOT: ON *Sally* AT ONE END OF THE TABLE. THIS IS A FAIRLY SMART LUNCH – SHE'S PUSHED THE BOAT OUT FOR *Mike* – BUT IN SOME WAYS THE SCENE SHOULD REFLECT THE BREAKFAST THAT OPENED THE WHOLE SERIES. SHE CLINKS A FORK AGAINST A GLASS.

Sally   Can I have your attention, please?

CUT TO: WIDER ANGLE. *John, Sally, Karen, Mike* AND *Steve* ARE AROUND THE TABLE. AT THE OPPOSITE END TO *Sally*, *John* OPENS A BOTTLE OF SPARKLING WINE.

Steve   What's that?

John   Sparkling wine.   [READS]   Methode Champenoise.

CAT-CALLS FROM AROUND THE TABLE.

Karen   Is that for Mike?

John   Well, it's a celebration. But not just 'cos Mike's home – although that's certainly something to celebrate.

Steve   Yeah. I'll drink to that.

Sally   Not at your age, you won't.

John   But this is also a celebration for me. And the zoo-packs.

Karen   Oh, no!

GROANS ALL ROUND. *John* RAISES A HAND.

John   All right. You may laugh. But I'm happy to say that a certain major hamburger chain disagrees.

Sally PRODUCES A FINISHED HAMBURGER CARTON – SIMILAR TO THE ONE WE SAW IN *Killers*.

Sally   We've just had our first order for them – twenty-five thousand of them, to be precise.

Karen OPENS HER MOUTH TO SPEAK.

John   And don't you start, Karen.

Karen   It's great, dad.

John   It means I'm in business for myself. My own car. My own boss. And that means a job for you, Mike. If you want it . . .

Mike   I don't know.

John   I'm not pushing you. You think about it. But that's what we're celebrating. All right?

Sally   No, it's not. Not just that. Not any of that.

> *Sally* RAISES HER GLASS.

Sally   We're together again, that's what really matters.

> *John* FILLS HER GLASS. IT FROTHS OVER THE EDGE.

Sally   Let's drink to the family.

> *John* FILLS THE OTHER GLASSES.

John   Yeah. The family. We're going to be all right.

> CUT TO:

SCENE SEVENTEEN
Int. Courtroom 3.00 p.m.

> THE SERIES CLOSES WHERE IT BEGAN – IN THE COURTROOM. THE *Magistrate* IS BEHIND HER DESK, AS EVER.

Magistrate   People like a happy ending. You've got to give them what they want.

> PULL BACK: TO REVEAL *Leo* TALKING TO THE *Magistrate* ON THE SET OF THE COURT. AND NOW IT IS JUST A SET. THIS IS THE ACTOR PLAYING *Leo* TALKING TO THE ACTRESS PLAYING THE *Magistrate*. WE CAN SEE THE CAMERAS AND LIGHTING EQUIPMENT BEHIND THEM.

Magistrate   How many more scenes have you got?

Leo   None. I got dropped out. I don't think they could find a happy ending for my character.

Magistrate   What are you doing next?

Leo   A 'Boon' – two weeks in Birmingham.

Magistrate   Is is a good part?

Leo   Black stereotype. White writer. Same old story . . .

THE *Producer's* VOICE (AS IN THE PREVIOUS PLAY) CALLS
OUT ACROSS THE DARKNESS

Producer   [v/o] All right, everyone. Can I have first positions?

Leo SHRUGS AND MOVES AWAY. THE *Magistrate*
STRAIGHTENS HERSELF UP.

Producer   [v/o] And . . .

CUT TO: CLOSE SHOT ON A CAMERA POINTING AT THE
Magistrate. THE RED LIGHT GLOWS.

CUT TO: BLACKOUT.

CUT TO: END CREDITS.

ACTIVITIES

A Piece of the Cake

■ THINKING ABOUT THE SITUATIONS

In groups Discuss these questions.

1 Was it right of John to fix up an interview for Mike without consulting him? Should Mike have agreed to go along to the interview for his dad's sake?

2 Was it wrong of Mike to throw away the wallet? What do you think his dad would say if he found out? How would his mum react?

3 Should Dave Pearson have warned John that the Q-T Pie doll factory was being taken over? What were his reasons for not doing so? If you had been Dave Pearson would you have said anything?

4 Why did Karen try to make an excuse not to go to the birthday tea? Was she wrong to do so? Why did Sally pressurise Karen into seeing her at lunch time? Was it fair of her to do so?

5 What do you think of what Mr Green says to Mike? Is it the sort of advice you'd expect a careers adviser to give? In what ways is Mr Green's conduct of the interview unconventional? Do you think he is the right sort of person to be a careers adviser, and to advise Mike?

6 What is the purpose of the short scene in which Steve is reading a passage from *Animal Farm*? Do you think it is helpful?

7 What do you think of the way the American chairman behaves? What do you think of his attitude to unions? Do you think there is any justification for his behaviour?

8 How does Dave Pearson behave towards the chairman? How does he feel after the interview? If you were in Dave Pearson's position, would you be prepared to do what the chairman asked?

9 Discuss what Sally says to Karen in Scene eighteen about why the family is important to her. What do you think of her views?

10 Was it wrong of Mike to make a remark about being approximately sixteen at his birthday tea? What do you think of the way Sally reacted? Was she right not to get involved in a discussion of Mike's adoption at that point?

11 Do you blame John for coming home slightly drunk that evening? Is it understandable, but inexcusable, that he had been drinking?

12 Do you think it was wrong of Mike to want to smoke in the house? Why did he bring the cigarettes out at that point? Whose decision should it be whether a teenager is allowed to smoke in the house?

13 What do you think of the way the various members of the family reacted to Sanjay's appearance? Think about the way in which this entrance is prepared for. Why is it so effective?

14 Why is this play called *A Piece of the Cake*?

■ THINKING ABOUT THE CHARACTERS

□ Mike

In pairs **1** What do you think of the way Mike behaves towards his parents and towards Steve in *A Piece of the Cake*? Do you think any of his behaviour is selfish or ungrateful? Why doesn't he want a job at the Q-T Pie doll factory? What is his attitude generally towards leaving school and finding a job?

2 Make a list of words to sum up your impression of Mike's character, based on his behaviour in this first play. What are his good points? What are his bad points? Find evidence from the script that supports your views, then form a group with two other pairs and compare and discuss your lists.

3 Think of Mike in other situations than those shown in this script. What would his bedroom be like – tidy or untidy? What posters would there be on the walls? What clothes would he have in his wardrobe? What magazines/comics, music, TV programmes and videos would he be interested in?
What is his best/weakest subject at school? How does he behave in class? What are his friends like, and what kind

of things do they like doing together? Note down your further ideas about Mike, then share them in a group discussion.

☐ Role plays

Is this yours?   Imagine that someone saw Mike throw away the wallet. They thought it looked suspicious, so they retrieved it and handed it in at the school office. Role play the scene in which the Head of Year asks Mike whether the wallet is his, and, if so, why he has thrown it away.

As a class   Draw up a list of questions you would like to ask Mike about his behaviour in *A Piece of the Cake*. Choose someone to take the 'hot-seat' as Mike and put these questions to him/her. Then, in a debriefing session, discuss the answers the person in the hot-seat gave.

On your own   1 Look at scene twenty-one. Imagine you are Mike. What are you thinking? Write down what you would say if you spoke your thoughts aloud.

2 Think about the sort of person Mike is at school. Write some of the comments that subject teachers might have written on his last report, then write the comment that his personal tutor might have written, summarising Mike's attitude and achievements during the previous three months.

☐ Being adopted

As it is his sixteenth birthday, Mike is thinking about the fact that he was adopted. For some people, the knowledge that they have been adopted does not concern them, but many adopted people are very anxious to know more about their backgrounds.

'I feel like a middle without a beginning. If you're not adopted you can't know what it's like to be shut out of a family's history. Who do I take after? Is there anyone out there like me?'   Daphne (herself adopted and the mother of adopted children).

Read Alison's story (p. 130). What do you learn from it about the feelings of an adopted person?

ALISON'S STORY

Alison is eighteen and has recently left home to work in a hotel in the Lake District, 300 miles from her parents. 'My adoptive parents,' as she firmly describes them. She is at pains to emphasise that she is not their natural daughter. 'I was adopted a long time ago – I can hardly remember it. In fact, for most of my childhood I did forget it and believed Sue and Terry were my proper parents. They certainly didn't go out of their way to help me keep in touch with my past.'

As a teenager, Alison had the usual arguments and periods of tension with her parents. It was only when an aunt remarked. 'Well, what do you expect when the girl is not really your own?', that the fact she had been adopted resurfaced. The more Alison asked questions about her past, the more upset and defensive her adoptive parents became.

'Maybe if they had talked more openly about it, it wouldn't have become so vital for me to learn where I really come from. But they hated me asking. I soon saw it was my only weapon. They could tell me what to do – do your homework, wash your face, turn the radio down – and all I had to do to get my own back was say that my real parents would have understood me properly. And I'd think about it, at night. What were they like – my mum and dad? Why did she give me up? Was it me, or was it that she couldn't afford to have a baby? Maybe she was young and couldn't marry my father. But what if she'd then grown up and married him – they couldn't have got me back because it was too late. So, they might be out there, just waiting for me to turn up. Well, now that's what I'm going to do. I'm going to get my birth certificate and I'm going to find them. I'm not expecting them to be rich or special or anything silly like that.

But they will be my parents and that's important to me.'

Alison feels strongly that she can't have a future until she has discovered her past. 'I don't know who I am, do I? I've got to go back into my real family to learn about the real me. I mean, all those years when I'd fill in forms at school that would ask me about my parents and family illnesses and things. It was all a lie, wasn't it? And those things make up your personality, so part of me is based on lies and I've got to find out the truth. When I find my mum and dad, it will fall into place and I'll be happy, I know I will. Perhaps then I can go back to Terry and Sue and thank them for looking after me – they did try their best. But I think you've got to have your own parents, don't you?'

If you're an adopted child ...

When adopted children reach eighteen (seventeen in Scotland), they now have the legal right to see their original birth certificate, and so find the means to trace their parents. If the adoption went through before 1976, this can only happen after a trained counsellor has talked to the adopted person.

Alison, for instance, will find that before she is given a copy of her full, original birth certificate with her real mother's name, address and occupation, and her original home (which may be different from her present one), she must talk at length to a social worker.

For children adopted after 1976, it is assumed that the new parents would have talked openly about such an event, and prepared the child for any contact if it is desired. Although the majority of adopted people want to know about their birth parents, only a few actually follow through to trace them.

☐ John

In pairs **1** What sort of person is John? Would you describe him as a traditional husband and father? What would you say are his strengths and weaknesses as (*a*) a father (*b*) a husband?

2 What is John's attitude towards work and the job that he has with Q-T Pie Dolls? Is his attitude different from Mike's simply because he is older, or is there a fundamental difference in their attitudes (through a difference of temperament, ambitions, etc.)?

3 What is your reaction to John? Do you like or dislike any particular feature of his character? Do you feel sympathy towards him at any point? Is he someone to whom you could relate?

What would it be like to have him as a father, as a husband or just a friend?

On your own

1 'I don't understand him, I really don't!' Imagine that, as he drives to work that morning after the scene at breakfast, John is thinking about Mike. Write down his thoughts.

2 Look at scene twenty, and imagine that you are John. Write down what you would say if you spoke your thoughts aloud.

☐ Sally

In pairs

1 What is your impression of Sally? Is she a strong personality? Point to evidence in her behaviour to support your view?

2 What sort of a wife and mother is Sally? What is her relationship with her husband, and with her daughter and sons? Do you think she understands her family? How much support does she give to John, and to her children?

☐ Role plays

Role play a scene in which a magazine reporter who is researching an article on 'A woman's place' interviews Sally and asks for her views on a woman's role. Sally explains why she chose to be a housewife rather than a career woman and what she feels is the importance of the family, and family life.

On your own

1 Imagine that Sally has a close friend who lives abroad now, but in whom she has always confided. Write the letter that she sends the following day, expressing her concerns about Mike and her fears for the future as a result of the impending closure of the Q-T Pie factory.

2 Imagine you are Sally. Write an article, 'A day in the life of Sally Williams', describing a typical day in your life.

☐ Steve

In pairs   **1** What is your impression of Steve? How is he different from his brother? Do your feelings about him change from the beginning to the end of *A Piece of the Cake*?

2 Think further about Steve, as you did about Mike (in the section above). Note down your ideas and share them in a group discussion.

On your own   **1** Imagine that Steve keeps a diary. Write the diary entry that Steve makes for Mike's birthday.

2 Look at scene twenty-two. Imagine that you are Steve. What are you thinking during this incident? Write what you would say if you spoke your thoughts aloud. Why do you think he is 'paralysed' during the argument?

☐ Karen

In pairs   **1** What impression do you get of Karen from the conversation she has with her mother? In what ways does she seem to be different from her brothers? What does the fact that she is a nurse suggest about her?

2 What do you imagine Karen thinks about her family? Role play a scene in which Karen talks to a new flatmate and tells her about her parents and her brothers. What are her hopes/fears for their futures?

☐ The Williams family

In groups   **1** Read scene two and scene twenty-two. Before you begin, pick out key points in the scene where it would be interesting to know exactly what the characters are thinking in addition to what they actually say. On television, of course, we get an insight into their thoughts by seeing their expressions and gestures, as well as hearing what they say. Provide such insights during your reading, by stopping the reading at these points and getting the people reading the parts to improvise and say what each person is thinking at those particular points.

2 'Close ups' and 'fades' are particular features of television/film scripts. What specific moments in *A Piece* *of the Cake* reflect the advantages of television production. Could it be a radio/stage play? What would be lost if it were turned into a radio or stage play?

☐ Role plays

During scene two, John comes close to losing his temper. On page 10 it says: 'John is on the edge of anger, but he doesn't want a row. He and his son have had too many . . .'. Suggest what John and Mike row about. In pairs, role play one of their rows.

Then, form groups of four and role play a row between John and Mike which takes place in front of Sally and Steve. Before you begin, discuss how Sally and Steve are going to react. Does Sally take her husband's or her son's side, or does she try, successfully or unsuccessfully, to steer a middle course and to defuse the situation? What does Steve do? Does he get involved on one side or the other, try to stir things up and exploit the situation, or does he become withdrawn, trying not to get involved?

It's Never Black and White

■ THINKING ABOUT THE SITUATIONS

In groups Discuss these questions.

1 Was McClintock right to end Mike's training placement? What motives did he have for doing so? If you were McClintock, what would you have done about Mike and the spark plug?

2 'It was Leo's fault. He shouldn't have asked Mike to get him a spark plug.'
'It was Mike's fault. He shouldn't have agreed to get one.'
Discuss these views.

3 Is there a difference between 'pilfering' and 'stealing'? Does it make a difference what you take, who from, or the value of the object?

4 McClintock takes cash from some customers so that he won't have to pay so much tax. What do you think of people who do this? Is taking the government's money different from taking something from a firm or an individual?

5 On what is McClintock's prejudice against black people based? Talk about stereotyping and how it arises. Read and discuss John Agard's poem, 'Stereotype' (below).

Stereotype

I'm a fullblooded
West Indian stereotype
See me straw hat?
Watch it good

I'm a fullblooded
West Indian stereotype
You ask
if I got riddum
in me blood
You going ask!
Man just beat de drum
and don't forget
to pour de rum

I'm a fullblooded
West Indian stereotype
You say
I suppose you can show
us the limbo, can't you?
How you know!
How you know!
You sure
you don't want me
sing you a calypso too
How about that

I'm a fullblooded
West Indian stereotype
You call me
happy-go-lucky
Yes that's me
dressing fancy
and chasing woman
if you think ah lie
bring yuh sister

I'm a fullblooded
West Indian stereotype
You wonder
where do you people
get such riddum
could it be the sunshine
My goodness
just listen to that steelband

Isn't there one thing
you forgot to ask
This native will answer
    anything
How about cricket?
I suppose you're good at it?
Hear this man
good at it!
Put de willow
in me hand
and watch me stripe
de boundary

Yes I'm a fullblooded
West Indian stereotype

that's why I
graduated from Oxford
    University
with a degree
in anthropology

6 'The only way to change people's attitudes is to have tougher laws against racial discrimination.' Discuss this view. How easy would it be to prove that McClintock discriminated against Leo because he is black? McClintock says, 'I've had people round from the council ...', but this doesn't seem to concern him. What does this say about the effectiveness of present legislation against racism?

7 Compare Frances Young's attitude towards being black with Leo's attitude. Is she right to criticise Leo for not picketing Sainsbury's or going on demonstrations to demand freedom for Nelson Mandela? Do you think it would help Leo, as she suggests, if he were to become more aware of his roots?

8 How is the poem used in scenes fifteen to twenty to show the viewer further insights into what life is like for Leo, a young black teenager growing up in England today? Discuss how the poet John Agard uses humour to make a number of serious points. How would you sum up this poem's message?

9 Mike complains that he is being exploited on this training scheme. Why? From what you know about training schemes, do you think they are a good idea or do you think young people who go on them are being exploited? Do you think young people should put up with some 'exploitation' in order to get training?

10 'Mike's act of vandalism is understandable but inexcusable.' Do you agree? Say why. How seriously do you view Mike's offence? If you were the magistrate, what punishment would you give him for breaking the window? Would it make a difference to your decision if you knew that he had been smoking a joint prior to committing the incident?

11 Why is the play given the title *It's Never Black and White*?

■ THINKING ABOUT THE CHARACTERS

□ Mike

In pairs 1 What do you learn about Mike in this play:
– from the way he behaves in the scenes with McClintock
– from his relationship with Leo; and
– from the decisions he makes about the spark plug, and throwing the brick through the window?

2 How has your view of Mike changed by the end of *It's Never Black and White* from the view you had of him at the end of the first play?

□ Role plays

1 The scene in which Mike tells his father about losing his place on the training scheme and his father calls him a thief.

2 A scene in which Mike explains to his YTS supervisor why McClintock has ended his placement.

3 A scene in which a social worker or probation officer talks to Mike and asks him to explain why he vandalised the window and to say what he feels about what has happened.

As a class Draw up a list of questions to ask Mike at the end of the play. Ask someone to take the hot-seat as Mike and question her/him. Then, in a debriefing session, discuss the answers the person in the hot-seat has given.

On your own Imagine you are Mike. When you get home that night, you cannot sleep because of the thoughts that are rushing through your head. Write down what you are thinking.

□ Leo

In pairs 1 What do you learn about Leo from the scene in which McClintock interviews him? What is your first impression of him?
   Do your ideas about Leo change as the play progresses? How does he react to McClintock's decision not to give him a job?

2 What is his relationship with his mother? Do you think he has a father, or brothers and sisters? If so, what are they like?

3 What do you learn about Leo from the scenes involving him and Mike? In their relationship, who is the more dominant figure – Leo or Mike? Why do you think they are friends?

4 Talk about Leo's background. His last job lasted five weeks. Suggest what it was and why it only lasted five weeks. He says he has been in trouble two years back – suggest what he has been in trouble for.

Discuss what you think Leo's bedroom is like. What sort of posters on the walls/clothes in the cupboards?

☐ Role plays

'How did it go then, Leo?' A black community worker, who knows Leo has been for a job interview, asks him how it went.

On your own
1 You are Leo. What thoughts are going through your head as your run off down the street at the end of the play?

2 During the interview, McClintock has Leo's CV in front of him. Brainstorm what you think is on Leo's CV, then write out a copy of it.

☐ McClintock

In pairs
1 Here are ten words that have been suggested to describe McClintock's character:

tough	arrogant
selfish	bigoted
obstinate	domineering
self-satisfied	ruthless
unscrupulous	intolerant

Can you suggest any others? Pick out four words which you think sum up the main features of McClintock's character and find evidence from the episode to support your views.

2 On page 47, Leo says of McClintock: 'I quite liked him'. What does Leo respect about McClintock? Discuss the positive aspects of McClintock's character.

☐ Role play

1 One of you is the director of *It's Never Black and White*; the other is the actor playing the part of McClintock.

Discuss together the impression you want to portray of McClintock.

2 *I bet I know who did it.* Role play a scene in which McClintock talks to a police officer the day after the incident and suggests that Mike is the culprit.

3 'What do you expect these days?' McClintock tells a friend – a self-made businessman like himself – about Mike, and explains and justifies his decision to end Mike's training and not to employ Leo. Has his friend had similar experience with trainees?

4 A scene in which a YTS supervisor talks to McClintock about Mike and discusses the decision to end Mike's training. (He has already received Mike's account of what happened.)

☐ **Frances**

In pairs **1** What is your impression of Leo's mother? How would you describe her relationship with her son? How helpful is her advice to him?

2 If you were playing the part of Frances Young in a production of this play, how would you try to portray her?

☐ **Role plays**

I can't get through to him. Frances Young talks to a friend, an artist like herself, about the problem she has in communicating her ideas to her son.

Killers

■ THINKING ABOUT THE SITUATIONS

In groups Discuss these questions.
1 What do you think of the way the magistrate questions John in scene one? Is John right to get angry? If you had been John, would you have become angry? For what reasons?

2 In what way was John breaking the law by picketing the Q-T Pie doll factory? Do you think he was right or wrong to do so?

3 Was it wrong of John to go into Mike's room without his permission? How much privacy is a young person entitled to at home? Does it depend, as John suggests, on who pays the bills?

4 What kind of crime is not paying for a meal in a fast food restaurant? How serious is such an offence? If you were a magistrate, what punishment would you give a teenager who committed such an offence? What 'extenuating circumstances' could you take into account before passing sentence?

5 What do you think of Mike's plan to rob an old lady? If he had suggested it to you, how would you have tried to persuade him against it? In pairs, role play a scene in which you try to persuade Mike to drop his plan.

6 Why is Karen so worried about the hole in the ozone layer? How concerned are you about the 'greenhouse effect' and acid rain? Read and discuss the articles below on these issues.

THE GREENHOUSE EFFECT

What's become known as the greenhouse effect is being caused by three main things

- **the build-up of CO_2 and other gases in the earth's atmosphere**
- **the destruction of the ozone layer**
- **the destruction of tropical rainforests**

Those gases

Since the beginning of the Industrial Revolution we have been burning great quantities of fossil fuel, like wood, coal and oil. Britain hasn't been alone. All the developed world has been doing this – and still is.

The carbon dioxide (CO_2) caused by this burning, lingers way above the earth's surface and, acting rather like a layer of double-glazing, is trapping heat and causing the world's temperature to rise.

● **Six billion tonnes of carbon dioxide from fossil fuels is belched into our atmosphere every year.**

But there are other gases too:

● **100 million tonnes of methane gas goes into the atmosphere each year from cows and sheep passing wind!**

● **Nitrous oxide from agricultural and garden fertilisers causes 6% of the problem.**

The ozone layer

You've no doubt heard that many aerosols are definitely taboo in a green lifestyle. The reason is that they contain chemicals called chlorofluorocarbons (CFCs), which are released into the atmosphere each time we press the squirt button. The CFCs drift upwards. When they reach the ozone layer they collect and erode this precious barrier that protects us from the ultra-violet rays of the sun. There is already a hole as big as America over the Antarctic.

CFCs also contribute to the green-house effect. CFCs can last up to 100 years, so even if they were banned now we still have problems in store for the future.

● **In the UK alone 800 million aerosols were produced last year.**

● **eighty per cent of them contained CFCs compared to ten per cent by the end of this year.**

● **CFCs also exist in fridges and freezers, take-away burger cartons, foam-filled furniture and are used to clean and maintain computer and electronic systems.**

The good news is ... twenty countries, including the UK, have agreed to phase out CFCs by the year 2000.

The bad news is ... our survival is still threatened. In the short term skin cancers could increase from the extra amount of ultra-violet rays entering our atmosphere. In the long term the effect on the production of crops and the food chain is unknown. If the ultra-violet rays start killing the first link in the food chain, called phytoplankton – tiny plants upon which all fish exist – then we will all be in trouble.

Tropical rainforests

Every time a tree is burned, CO_2 goes into the atmosphere, and given that an area larger than England is being destroyed every year the problem is massive.

The tropical rainforests play an important role in the world's climate. Mile upon mile of a glorious, natural wonderland, full of beautiful animals and magnificent plants and trees is being brutally and wantonly destroyed. Why? For money.

The rainforests fall within third world countries. These countries all have weak economies and they are grossly in debt to the developed world.

● **Third world countries owe the first world over 1000 billion US dollars, a huge sum.**

Some countries, like Indonesia, are chopping down their trees to sell the wood to Japan who actually buy forty per cent of all the tropical rain forest timber for chopsticks!

Other countries, like those in Latin America, are clearing the trees for cattle grazing – exporting beef is very profitable.

But the clearing is a suicide mission anyway, for the land will only be fit for grazing for about ten years. By then the heavy torrential rains will have eroded the soil – which once was held together by trees – so much that it will be fit for nothing.

'But the real tragedy', says Dr Jeremy Leggett, Greenpeace's director of science, 'is that we are losing so many species. The rainforests are the power houses of evolution, there are many species there we haven't yet discovered. Many can help with health problems.'

ACID RAIN

Acid rain is caused by several things:
- **The burning of fossil fuels in our power stations**
- **The burning of fossil fuel in heavy industry**
- **The nitrogen oxide which comes from car exhausts.**

The sulphur and nitrogen oxides enter the air, float upwards into the atmosphere and eventually fall down again as rain, mist or snow.

Sometimes they will have travelled great distances which means one country's burning can cause another country's acid rain. The result is:
- **Massive damage to forests and woodlands. Britain is the worst affected country in Europe – some fifty-six per cent of our trees are unhealthy. As Andrew Tickle of Greenpeace says 'Whole areas of forest are declining, many trees are dying.' There are also problems in Germany, Switzerland, the Nether-** lands, USSR and Denmark.
- **Lakes become acidified, killing fish and fauna. Scandinavia and Britain are badly affected.**
- **Buildings are corroded by the acidity. York Minster, Cologne Cathedral and London's St Paul's Cathedral are among the list of Europe's damaged buildings.**
- **Agricultural land can become too acidic which means farmers use more and more chemical fertilisers to obtain the crop yield they need.**

The good news is ... the British government has just bowed to European pressure and by 1992 the majority of cars will be produced with converters on their exhaust systems which will stop the release of the harmful nitrogen oxide.

The bad news is ... by 1994 only one of Britain's forty-one guilty power stations will have been given filters.

7 What do you think of the activities of pressure groups such as Greenpeace and Friends of the Earth? What do you know about the Green Party and its policies? Would you consider joining these organisations or voting for the Green Party? What is your view of people who campaign about green issues?

8 Is it hypocritical of Karen to criticise her father and yet to drive a car herself? Should John abandon his business project because of the harmful effects that styrofoam has on the environment? If you were in John Williams' position, what would you do? What do you think is the government's role in protecting our environment?

9 *'Any job is better than no job.'* Talk about the job Leo has to do in the fast food restaurant. How is it different from the job he would really like to do? In Leo's situation, what would you do – take the job available or continue to draw the dole?

10 Why is the play called *Killers*? Find all the references to killing in the play and discuss the reasons why it is given that title.

■ THINKING ABOUT THE CHARACTERS

□ Mike

In pairs   **1** Suggest what Mike's thoughts and feelings are during and after the conversation in which his father accuses him of stealing the stereo.

2 What do you think Mike is thinking while the magistrate questions his father? Do you think he blames his father for what has happened?

3 What do you learn about Mike from his conversations with Leo in *Killers*? What does Mike say to Leo about life being a game and what do you think makes him decide to break the rules?

4 What do you learn about Mike from his conversation with Steve in scene eighteen? Mike says: 'I may be stupid, but I'm not as thick as all that.' What does he mean? Do you think he *is* either 'stupid' or 'thick'? Give your reasons.

5 Suggest what Mike is thinking during the celebration dinner.

6 Judging by his behaviour in this play, do you think Mike is a strong or a weak character? Say why.

7 *'It is easier to understand Mike's behaviour than to sympathise with it.'* Discuss this view. How far do you sympathise with Mike at the end of this play?

□ Role plays

'You're heading for trouble, you are.' A scene in which a youth club worker tries to offer Mike some friendly advice, because he suspects Mike is becoming more reckless. How does Mike react to this attempt to influence him?

On your own   Choose one of the incidents involving Mike and write an account of it, describing it from Mike's point of view. Then, write an account of it from someone else's point of view, for example, his father's or Leo's. When you have finished, form groups and discuss the different accounts you have written. How many conflicts in this, and the two previous plays, do you think are the result of people's failure to appreciate each other's views.

☐ John

In pairs   **1** What effect has being made redundant had on John? Why did he join in the picketing of the factory, even after the company had obtained a court injunction? How does this action compare with Mike's stealing of the spark plug in *A Piece of the Cake?*

2 How did John feel after the picketing collapsed? Discuss what he says to Sally in scene fifteen. How have his attitudes changed since the first play?

3 Talk about how John behaves in this play. What sort of an example do you think he sets to Mike by his behaviour?

4 By the end of the play, has your attitude to John changed in any way from the attitude you had towards him at the end of *A Piece of the Cake?*

☐ Role plays

1 (a) A scene in which a reporter interviews John during the picketing and asks him to explain why he is picketing the factory.
(b) A similar interview, after the picketing has been called off, in which the reporter asks John for his views on the settlement that has been agreed.

2 'He'd no right to question me like that!' John complains to Sally about the way the magistrate questioned him.

3 A continuation of scene four, in which John tries to apologise for suspecting that Mike stole the stereo. Will Mike accept his apology?

4 After the celebration dinner, John talks to Sally about Karen's attitude to his new business scheme. Do you think he is more patient with his daughter, than with his sons?

As a class   Draw up a list of questions to ask John at the end of this play. Ask someone to hot-seat being John and question her/him. Then, in a debriefing session, discuss the answers the person in the hot-seat has given.

ACTIVITIES

On your own Imagine that John keeps a diary. Write a series of entries, describing his thoughts and feelings (a) after a day's picketing (b) on the day the picketing was called off (c) after the conversation in which he accuses Mike of stealing the stereo (d) after the meeting at which the proposal for the zoo-packs is given a government grant (e) after the celebration dinner.

□ Leo

In pairs 1 What do you learn about Leo from the way he reacts (a) when Mike first suggests robbing Maggie Lambert (b) when Mike runs off from the fast food restaurant without paying?

2 Why does Leo decide to take a job waiting? What are his feelings about the job once he has started?

3 Suggest the thoughts that are passing through Leo's mind (a) in scene twenty-four as he hesitates before deciding to join in the robbery with Mike (b) in scene thirty-one, as he runs off.

□ Role plays

Leo retells the story of the break-in to someone he trusts not to say anything, explaining why he agreed to take part and describing how he felt during it and immediately afterwards.

□ Karen

In pairs 1 What does the fact that Karen is concerned about the environment tell you about her?

2 Discuss the way Karen stands up to her father and tells him what she feels about styrofoam and its effects. Do you think it is wrong of her to do so at the celebration dinner?

□ Role plays

A scene in which Karen tells her flatmate what she discovered about her father's business idea at the celebration dinner. Does her flatmate feel John's arguments are reasonable?

144

On your own Imagine you are Karen. Use the information in the articles about the greenhouse effect and acid rain and compose a letter to the local newspaper, expressing your concern about the damage being done to the environment, and suggesting improvements at a local level that could be implemented.

As Seen on TV

■ THINKING ABOUT THE SITUATIONS

In groups Discuss these questions.

1 What impressions of Maggie Lambert and the attack on her are Carrie Andrews and her producer trying to create in scene one? Talk about the emotive language that Carrie uses and the visual images that the producer uses in order to create those impressions.

2 In scene 5, Mike and Leo discuss what to do. At one point, Mike suggests that they should go to the police. Do you think they should have given themselves up? Give your reasons.

3 Why does Leo mistrust the police? In your opinion, is he right to be wary of the police? What evidence can you quote to support your views? Why is it very unlikely that Leo will be treated roughly, as he fears, by the police?

4 What images of the police are given in *Killers* – in the TV programme Mike and Steve watch, in Leo's dream, in the montage sequences and in the scenes involving Colin Firth? Talk about how our images of the police are formed. What is your image of the police? On what is this based – first-hand experience? Hearsay? What you have read in the newspapers, or seen on TV?

5 Discuss the reaction of the people on the housing estate when they open their doors during the house-to-house enquiries. Why are they mistrustful and unwilling to get involved? Suggest what the police officers must feel when they meet this reaction.

6 Discuss the comments made by the police officers during the montage sequence, all of which were made to the author in interviews with police officers in Hackney.

What do your learn from them about the police and their attitudes?

What role do you think the police ought to play in society? How do you think they could improve their image?

7 Was it wrong of Steve to go into Mike's room and to look through his things? When he found the pension book, should he have gone to the police?

8 Was it unfair of Steve to make Sonia promise not to say anything, then to tell her about the pension book? Was she wrong to go to the headmaster? If you had been Sonia, what would you have done?

9 Talk about the way Carrie interviews Firth and the way he reacts to her. Do you think her attitude and her questions are fair? Is she just doing her job or is her behaviour irresponsible?

10 What do you learn about Maggie from what Joyce Lambert says about her? How different is the picture Joyce gives of Maggie from the stereotypical image of her that is presented in scene one? Why does the producer decide not to include the true facts about Maggie in any of his reports?

11 What do you think of the way the interview with Joyce was edited before it was broadcast? Do you regard such editing as (a) very clever journalism (b) highly irresponsible and immoral behaviour (c) typical – and inevitable – news reporting? How easy is it for viewers to tell whether or not a TV interview has been edited?

12 How is Maggie's funeral presented on TV? Talk about the way Carrie introduces it – the questions she asks and the language she uses. How do she and her producer present the situation in order to put across their own messages?

13 Discuss how the writer, Anthony Horowitz, uses the sequences of short scenes twenty-nine to forty-six, involving the presentation of Maggie's funeral and the parody of the TV police chase, to show how television can distort reality.

14 Why is this play called *As shown on TV*?

□ Role plays

In pairs A telephone conversation between a radio presenter and a listener who has telephoned a radio programme called 'On the Line' to express her/his views on the Maggie Lambert affair, based on the TV reports she/he has seen.

As a class Role play a TV studio discussion in which a panel of experts and a studio audience express their concerns about incidents where old people, like Maggie Lambert, are the victims of burglaries and assaults, and discuss why they think such incidents occur, what can be done to prevent them and how to deal with any offenders who are caught. Start by choosing someone to act as presenter and two or three people to act as experts. Then, before you begin, decide on roles for various members of the audience. Tape record or video the discussion, so that you can refer to what was said in a debriefing session afterwards.

On your own **1** Write newspaper reports for two different newspapers the day after the break-in, while Maggie is lying in hospital, critically ill. Write one report in a sensational style, exploiting the opportunity to arouse readers' emotions, and the other in a much more restrained style, giving only the facts and avoiding wild speculations.

2 How are the police presented on TV? In groups, talk about the image of the police that is given in programmes such as 'The Bill'. How does this compare with the image given by the more glamorous, 'action-packed' series such as 'Cagney and Lacey' and 'Hill Street Blues'. Then, each write an essay on the way the police are portrayed on television. Use the title: 'Images of the police'.

■ THINKING ABOUT THE CHARACTERS

□ Leo and Mike

In pairs **1** In what ways do Leo's and Mike's attitudes differ in scene eight? Imagine that one of you is Leo and the other is Mike. Write down what you are thinking as you go off alone at the end of the scene. Then, discuss together what you have written.

2 What do you learn about Mike and the reasons for his behaviour from what he tells Leo in the scene in the breakers' yard? When he says 'Oh Leo . . .' at the end of the scene, what is he thinking?

3 In scene twenty-eight, why won't Leo tell Firth who was with him? Is Leo right or wrong not to say anything?

□ Role plays

In pairs 1 A scene after his arrest in which Leo's mother visits him.

2 The scene at the police station in which Firth questions Mike about what happened at Maggie's.

In threes A scene after Mike's arrest in which Sally and John visit him.

□ Derek, Sonia and Steve

In pairs 1 What do you learn about Derek's attitudes from what he says to Sonia in scene nine? What sort of person is Derek? What do you think of him and his attitudes? Is he the sort of person you would like to be friendly with?

2 Compare Sonia's behaviour in this play with her behaviour in *A Piece of the Cake*. Talk about why she behaves differently towards Steve. How would you describe Sonia? Each write a short pen-portrait of her, then discuss what you have written.

3 Discuss the way Steve behaves in *As Seen on TV*. Has your impression of Steve changed in any way by the end of the play? If so, how has it changed and why?

□ Role plays

1 Derek talks to one of his mates after his conversation with Sonia and expresses the view that 'she's going soft'.

2 Sonia swears a friend to secrecy, then tells her why she decided to go to tell the Head. How does the friend react – does she tell Sonia that she did the right thing?

3 Each play the part of Steve. Role play the conversation he might have had with himself in his head as he debated whether or not to tell anybody what he has discovered. One Steve argues that he should tell somebody, the other Steve argues that he should keep quiet.

On your own Imagine that Sonia keeps a diary. Write the entries that she makes (a) after talking to Derek (b) after going to the skating rink (c) after Steve tells her about the pension book (d) after she has spoken to the Head.

☐ Karen

In pairs If Steve had confided in Karen in scene twenty-seven, what would she have suggested he should do? Improvise and then script an alternative ending to the scene, using this idea.

On your own Imagine you are Karen. Write a monologue in which Karen speaks her thoughts aloud as she leaves the cemetery.

Judgements

■ THINKING ABOUT THE SITUATIONS

In groups Discuss these questions.

1 *'Mike needs a short, sharp shock.'* Discuss this view. What is your opinion of the sentence which the magistrate gives Mike? Is it too harsh/too lenient/the right sentence? What sentence would you have given Mike?

2 Do you think Mike will benefit from six months' you[?] custody? Discuss the view that he would benefit far m[?]e from a non-custodial sentence involving community service.

3 Who do you think is to blame for Mike getting into trouble – Mike himself? His parents? His school – for failing to interest and to discipline him? Society, because it failed to provide him with a job that would have kept him out of trouble?

4 It has been suggested that parents of young people who get into trouble should be made to accept more responsibility for their children's actions. What do you think of this idea? Do you think, in Mike's case, involving his parents would help to keep him out of further trouble?

5 Leo's case is being treated separately from Mike's. Is it right that two people accused of the same crime can

sometimes be tried separately? Is Leo more to blame for what happened, because he is older than Mike and should have known better, or less to blame, because it was Mike's idea?

6 We never know what sentence Leo is given. Can you suggest why we are not told? If you were the magistrate, what sentence would you give Leo?

7 Derek's response when Steve stands up to him is to challenge Steve to a fight. What do you think of fighting as a way of dealing with arguments and differences of opinion? If someone insults you, or says something about you behind your back, what other ways of dealing with it are there besides fighting?

8 Discuss how the play ends. Why do you think the author, Anthony Horowitz, ends by reminding viewers that it is just a story? Do you think it spoils the effect of the play to be reminded, at the end, that it is all just a story?

9 Why is the episode called *Judgements*? Find all the references to judging that occur in the script and list all the different judgements that are being made in the play.

In pairs Script an extra scene, to be included after Mike has been sentenced, in which Carrie prepares a TV report, first reminding viewers of the events leading to Maggie's death, then reporting the sentence given to Mike, before interviewing a local councillor who is disgusted with the sentence and thinks that there should be tougher penalties for 'young layabouts'.

On your own 'Custody's not the answer', says a youth worker. Write an article for the local newspaper with this headline, reporting the views of a youth worker who argues that non-custodial sentences are the best way to help young offenders.

■ THINKING ABOUT THE CHARACTERS

□ John

In pairs 1 How does John react when Mike is sentenced to six months' youth custody? Discuss why he reacts this way. Do you think he should be more supportive of his son, whatever his opinion of his actions?

2 How is John's behaviour towards Mike different when he goes to pick him up on his release? Why has his attitude towards his son changed? How deep do you think this goes?

3 What mistakes do you think John has made in the past when dealing with Mike? How successful do you think he is likely to be in the future in trying to build a different relationship with Mike?

□ Sally

1 How is Sally's reaction to Mike's sentence different from her husband's? What does Sally reveal about her character by the way she reacts to John's attitude towards Mike's sentence?

2 At the end of the plays, despite everything, the Williams family is still together as a unit. How much is this due to Sally? Compare your view of Sally at the end of *Judgements* with your view of her at the end of *A Piece of the Cake*. In what way is it different, and why?

□ Mike

1 Suggest what Mike is thinking when he hears that he has been sentenced to six months' youth custody.

2 Why does Mike break out of custody? What is he planning to do? Suggest what his thoughts and feelings are as he leaves Leo's home, after Leo has told him he doesn't want to see him again.

3 At the end of the play, do you think Mike has learned his lesson? Will he be able to establish a new and better relationship with his father? Do you think he will accept his father's offer of a job? Do you think he *should* do?

☐ Steve

1 Talk about the way Steve deals with Derek. What aspects of Steve's character are revealed by this?

2 What is your final impression of Steve? How has it changed from your first impression of him? Why has it changed?

☐ Karen

Suggest what Karen is thinking and feeling during the dinner party (scene twenty).

☐ Role plays

In pairs A scene after the celebration dinner in which Steve asks Mike how he is, what it was like in custody and what he plans to do now that he is out.

As a class Choose five people to be the members of the Williams family and hot-seat them together. Ask them questions about what has happened to them over that year and how they feel about it. Tape record their answers so that you can refer to them in the debriefing session.
Then, choose another five people to be the Williams family in five years' time. Question them about what has happened in their lives during those five years.

On your own **1** Sally writes a letter to the same friend to whom she wrote after *A Piece of the Cake* (see page 131). She describes the eventful year which the family have had and her feelings about what has happened, and what the future holds.

2 Imagine you are Steve. At school, you are set a GCSE assignment to write a story entitled 'The turning point', describing an autobiographical experience. You write the story of how you turned the tables on Derek.

☐ Leo

In pairs **1** Why is Leo so angry when his mother visits him at the police station? How well do you think she handles the visit? How much notice does he take of what she says? Suggest what he is thinking at the end of their conversation.

2 What does Leo say when Mike visits him while he is on the run? What do you think has caused Leo's attitude to change? Do you think he should be more loyal to Mike?

☐ Role plays

'*I was just a kid. I did some pretty stupid things.*' A scene in which Leo, aged twenty-five, talks to a friend about the trouble he got into as a teenager.

☐ Derek and Sonia

1 What does the way Derek talks to Sonia about Steve and the things he says to Steve reveal about Derek?

2 How will being humiliated by Steve affect Derek? Do you think it will make him change his behaviour in any way?

3 What do you think of people like Derek? Have they any positive points? What sort of adult do you think he will grow into unless he changes his attitudes and behaviour?

4 What is your final impression of Sonia? How would you describe her behaviour in this play? Why does she feel it necessary to tell Steve about what she did? Is Steve right when he says: 'It doesn't matter any more'? Do you think she should be at the celebratory dinner?

On your own Write a further set of entries for Sonia's diary. Include entries describing her thoughts and feelings (a) after the showdown at the ice rink (b) after she confesses to Steve that she broke her promise.

Starting Out

■ THINKING ABOUT THE FIVE PLAYS

Read Anthony Horowitz's introduction.

In groups 1 Talk about the reservations Anthony Horowitz had when he was asked to write the series. In the end, why did he decide to write the plays?

2 Do you think Anthony Horowitz succeeded in writing a gripping story? Which of the five plays in the book did you find the most gripping? Explain why.

3 How successful is Anthony Horowitz in his attempts to reveal how the story is told in a television drama series? Discuss how he uses effects such as captions, dream sequences, montage sequences, flashbacks, subtitles, voice overs, satire, parody and exaggeration to remind viewers that they are watching a TV drama and not a real-life story. In which of the plays do you think these techniques are used most effectively?

4 Do you think Anthony Horowitz manages to avoid putting across a particular point of view about the issues he raises in his plays? Does his presentation of any of the characters or issues make you angry? If so, why?

5 Discuss the two questions Anthony Horowitz has often asked himself: (a) Is Sally a stereotype? (b) Is it wrong of TV producers, teachers and publishers to censor the language in television programmes and books?

6 What conclusion does Anthony Horowitz reach at the end of his introduction? Do you think he is right? What have you learned about the power and influence of television, and about how TV drama works, from seeing and reading the *Starting Out* scripts?